DISCOVERING ART SERIES

Twentieth Century Art

by Michael Batterberry

Foreword by Howard Conant
New York University

McGRAW-HILL BOOK COMPANY

New York • San Francisco • Toronto

Also in paperback in the Discovering Art Series:

GREEK & ROMAN ART adapted by Ariane Ruskin and Michael Batterberry
NINETEENTH CENTURY ART adapted by Ariane Ruskin
SEVENTEENTH & EIGHTEENTH CENTURY ART adapted by Ariane Ruskin

In hardcover:

CHINESE AND ORIENTAL ART, adapted by Michael Batterberry
GREEK & ROMAN ART, adapted by Ariane Ruskin and Michael Batterberry
NINETEENTH CENTURY ART, adapted by Ariane Ruskin
SEVENTEENTH & EIGHTEENTH CENTURY ART, adapted by Ariane Ruskin
TWENTIETH CENTURY ART, by Michael Batterberry
ART OF THE EARLY RENAISSANCE, adapted by Ariane Ruskin
ART OF THE HIGH RENAISSANCE, adapted by Ariane Ruskin
PREHISTORIC ART AND ANCIENT ART OF THE NEAR EAST, adapted by Ariane Ruskin
ART OF THE MIDDLE AGES, adapted by Michael Batterberry
PRIMITIVE ART, adapted by Ariane Ruskin and Michael Batterberry

Acknowledgment is hereby given to Purnell & Sons Ltd. for the right to base this work on the text of the magazine series, "Discovering Art" and to Fratelli Fabbri Editori for the right to make adaptions from the Italian text of *Capolavori Nei Secoli.*

Library of Congress Catalog Card Number: 73-1443

FOREWORD

by Howard Conant

Professor and Chairman, Department of Art Education; and Head, Division of Creative Arts, New York University

THE STYLE and content of Michael Batterberry's adaptation of *Twentieth Century Art* is as provocative and elucidating as the brilliant, staccato-beat manifestos of the futurists, surrealists, and others described in his text. Augmented by a large and very fine collection of color illustrations, Mr. Batterberry's treatment of the visual arts of the twentieth century is praiseworthy both for its excellent content and the contemporary sparkle of its style.

Traditional art historians often look upon modern artists as old-fashioned adults look upon modern youth: with dismay or with a lack of understanding. Mr. Batterberry's orientation is antithetical to that of the traditional historian; yet his scholarship is impeccable and he never reverts to the unpleasant practice of building a case for one art period at the expense of another. Most histories of art pay little more than lip service to modern art, if indeed they include it at all. Mr. Batterberry not only gives the artists and art works of this century the thoughtful attention they deserve; but he has produced one of the best-written, best-illustrated, and most comprehensive critical histories of twentieth-century art in the category of comprehensive period texts.

One of the most appealing characteristics of *Twentieth Century Art* is its in-depth analysis of major styles, schools, movements, and individual artists' works, accompanied in most cases by several large, full-color illustrations. Readers will be pleased to find that volumes in the "Discovering Art Series" thoughtfully avoid the encyclopedic boredom of art books which mention everything but tell and illustrate little or nothing. *Twentieth Century Art* is, in fact, a substantial volume, and it does provide ample opportunity for the author to deal with little-known but nevertheless important art movements and styles such as the "Section d'Or," "Peintres Maudits," "Jugendstil," and "Intimism."

Speaking of "youth style" (Jugendstil), Mr. Batterberry's book has plenty of it. Readers are bound to read his accounts of the lives of rebellious, impatient, and talented young people with fixed interest. Also interesting is the fact that these rebellious, often misunderstood, youngsters bore such names as Picasso and Modigliani. But even more worthy of consideration is the fact that these anti-social, rebellious youngsters produced, both during their youth and in later years, some of the greatest artistic masterworks of the twentieth century. Like some of today's youthful rebels, Picasso, Modigliani, and their friends were "turned on," highly productive radicals rather than "turned off" indolents.

Mr. Batterberry's *Twentieth Century Art* is admirably suited as a text for art survey and humanities courses. To choose a less profound, less comprehensive, and less well-illustrated text for such courses would certainly be ill advised. *Twentieth Century Art* will make a valuable and interesting addition to the home library; but better still would be individual acquisitions of the entire "Discovering Art Series." Needless to say, the same recommendation applies to school and community libraries.

CONTENTS

Introduction

FOR MANY generations, the very mention of Paris has been sufficient to excite the imagination. According to variations in personal taste and interests, Paris has been immediately associated with high fashion and low life, magnificent food and starving Bohemians, grandeur and gaiety, frivolous women, witty intellectuals, and the constant celebration of the arts. This reputation has probably never been so justified as during the period called "La Belle Époque" (meaning "the beautiful era" or, less literally, "the good old days"), which lasted from about 1885 to the eve of World War I in 1914.

By the turn of the century the city had become, among other things, the international capital of daring experimental art. The impressionists such as Renoir, Monet, and Degas had paved the way by breaking once and for all with stuffy academic traditions and pursuing their own bold and colorful course. Yet, in their time, they had by no means been universally accepted by the average gallerygoer as modern masters, in the way that established present-day artists are now looked upon by critics and the public. Foreign artists came to learn from the impressionists, but many tourists and ordinary viewers who failed to understand the new movement sniggered and laughed.

Not until the great Paris World's Fair of 1900 was such a "modern" genius as the sculptor Auguste Rodin (1840–1917) given proper recognition, at a large government-sponsored pavilion where his works were exhibited exclusively. The Paris exposition lasted from April to October, and a brief description of it may conjure up some of the charm and activity of the period.

Had the experienced traveler not been forewarned of the exceptional circumstances, he might easily have been dumbfounded by the appearance of Paris in 1900. Granted that he could still rediscover a favorite café near the serenely gaudy Opera House or gape at the world's most renowned beauties on their morning drives through the Bois de Boulogne, their enormous eyes and jewels glinting busily in the wine bottle shadows. He could still recapture his first shiver of giddiness while peeking out from the geometric metal lace high atop the Eiffel Tower. Once he was safely back on the ground, however, this dizzying sensation might understandably be replaced by an equally unnerving one of having awakened on the wrong continent, for suddenly he would find himself, according to French diplomat and novelist Paul Morand, in "that Arab, Negro, and Polynesian land that stretched from the Eiffel Tower to Passy, a Parisian slope that suddenly carried on its back Africa and Asia." The attractions of this exotic dream-world included a Ceylonese pavilion where one could loll about sipping iced tea while watching the devil dancers, a Tonkinese village complete with betel-chewing natives, a Tunisian bazaar, and an ingenious "train trip" to China in a fur-strewn Trans-Siberian railway car.

While the many European exhibits were planned to satisfy a multitude of interests, the underlying theme of the exposition was the "modern style," which at that time still meant Art Nouveau ("New Art"). This was a decorative style characterized by nervous, swirling lines which was most successfully applied in furniture, jewelry (Plate 1), ceramics, typography, and book illustration

1. French pendant typifying Art Nouveau style, gold and enamel

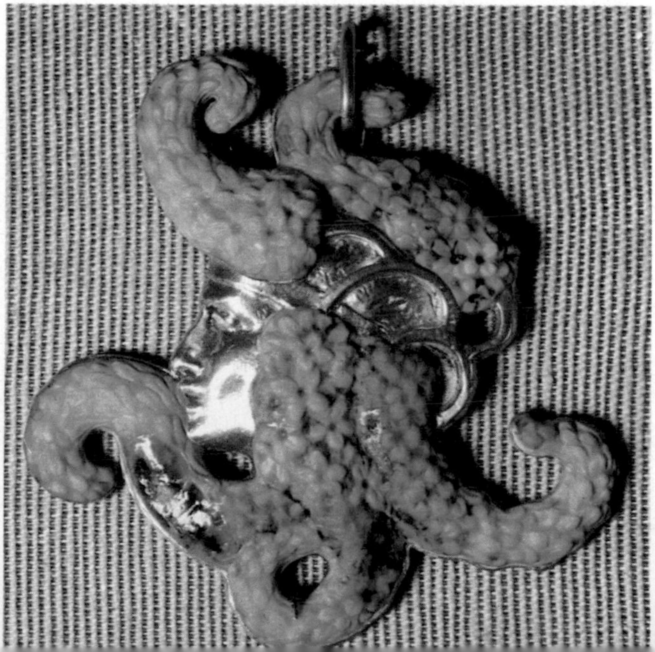

and posters. Its influence has lately reappeared in the writhing curves of psychedelic poster art and design. Paul Morand observed humorously that the original inspirations for Art Nouveau were "the gourd, the pumpkin, and the marshmallow . . . then one piled on the hydrangea, the bat, the tuberose and the peacock feather."

Millions came to the World's Fair, and numbered among the swarming crowds were princes and dukes, as well as famous statesmen and theatrical celebrities. The Parisian throngs took no particular notice of a young Spaniard with the face of a bullfighter who had just arrived on his first trip to Paris. They might have done well to do so, however, because it was he, Pablo Picasso, who would soon embalm the outmoded artistic traditions to which they stubbornly clung. But it must not be assumed that the following years were to be dominated artistically by Picasso alone, for this was to be the era of the twentieth-century giants—those who were responsible for one of the most significant, vital, and explosive periods in the history of world art. Truly, it would be but a pale understatement to say that never before, in such a short span of time, was the direction of painting and sculpture so violently altered.

And who, in turn, had been directly—or even indirectly—responsible for these brash young innovators? Some art historians and critics have called Paul Cézanne (1839–1906) "the father of modern art," but this convenient solution leaves the background of too many of the new movements unexplained. Cézanne himself said that art was a matter of theory developed and applied in contact with nature. More specifically, he meant that nature should be interpreted "through the cylinder, the sphere, the cone, with everything in proper perspective, so that each side of an object, of a plane, recedes toward a central point." He felt that a work of art should be organized like a completed architectural monument, but that we should not be aware of its separate parts. This emphasis on structure can be easily detected in the geometrically sturdy portrait of Cézanne's noted art dealer, Ambroise Vollard (Plate 2). Actually, what Cézanne was doing when applying his theories

2. ***Portrait of Ambroise Vollard,*** **by Paul Cézanne**

to painting was "thinking" with his eyes, an approach that was to influence greatly a later school called "cubism."

Equally influential in the development of other phases of twentieth-century art were Vincent van Gogh (1853–1890) and Paul Gauguin (1848–1903). Of somewhat lesser importance were Edvard Munch, (1863–1944), James Ensor (1860–1949), and Odilon Redon (1840–1916). Following a retrospective exhibition arranged by Roger Fry in London in 1910, Cézanne, Van Gogh, and Gauguin, along with others of their general period, came to be known as "post-impressionists." Before this, the term "expressionist" had been coined to describe Van Gogh. It suggests that his distorted images (Plate 3), which vibrate with a frantic life and color, were meant to express a strong emotion that would make the viewer *feel* along with the artist, rather than just *see*. In this subjective aim, Van Gogh differed from the impressionists, who, regardless of their rebellious attitudes, sought primarily to capture a visual experience in terms of natural light and color. Deep sentiments were generally ignored by them, in favor of fleeting impressions that would leave the viewer pleased and comfortably undisturbed (Plate 4). How different from the tortured paintings of the Norwegian Edvard Munch. His typically gloomy *Summer Night at Oslofjord* (Plate 5) must definitely be considered expressionistic. A forlorn, solitary little figure that is suggested by two or three brushstrokes, some animate and menacing trees, and the horrendous mouthlike island in the background all help to communicate an extremely sinister and lonely feeling.

Gauguin called himself a "symbolist." Basically, the term "symbolism" denotes that one thing suggests, recalls, or represents another. Symbols themselves can take innumerable forms. They may be as familiar and obvious as the skull and crossbones on a bottle of poison or as spiritual as the dove representing the Holy Ghost. The symbolism of various colors is so widely accepted that their meanings are taken for granted: for example, the direct association between the white bridal gown and purity, the red rose and love, and the black veil and sorrow. (It should be noted that color symbolism may vary from one culture or era to another.) Moreover, each of us has personal reactions to colors, shapes, or situations, and thus we come to form our own private associations. The painters known as symbolists used such personal symbols in form and color, to convey particular moods or private visions to others.

Gauguin's symbolism consisted of using color freely (that is, boldly and subjectively) rather than realistically. "What beautiful ideas," he exulted, "can be conjured up by form and color, now that we have no religious painting." He argued that, if one wished to paint a beautiful tree, why not use the most pure and brilliant green to represent it? In other words, why dull a bright color

3. *Portrait of Doctor Gachet,* by Vincent van Gogh

4. *Water Lilies,* by Claude Monet

straight from the tube by mixing it with another simply to imitate nature? One thinks of a tree as being green, so let it be the most arresting and undiluted hue.

Nevermore (Plate 6), which takes its title and the watchful bird from Edgar Allen Poe's poem "The Raven," bears out theses ideas,

5. ***Summer Night at Oslofjord,*** **by Edvard Munch**

notwithstanding the painting's deliberately somber tones. Of this picture Gauguin wrote, "I have tried to suggest a certain bygone barbaric luxury in a single nude. . . . It is neither silk nor velvet nor batiste nor gold that creates this luxurious quality, but simply a richness created by the hand of the artist." Among the many

6. *Nevermore,* by Paul Gauguin

artists influenced by the freedom of Gauguin's color and the flatly patterned surfaces of his pictures were Picasso and Henri Matisse (1869–1954).

Another important symbolist, Odilon Redon, frequently used a broad range of shimmering color to create a fantasy world of flowers, winged horses, mysterious men in the moon, and mythological beings. Even in the delicate and relatively straightforward *Portrait of the Artist's Son Ari* (Plate 7), one is struck by an indefinable and haunting air of unreality. It is this visionary or dreamlike quality of Redon's art which foreshadows a later movement called "surrealism."

Van Gogh, Gauguin, and Cézanne shared admirable traits of uncommon artistic integrity and courage. A degree of recognition finally came to Cézanne during his lifetime, but the earlier years of rejection by critics and public had by then left him painfully scarred. Gauguin died in lonely squalor, after having tried vainly to commit suicide in the jungle. Van Gogh, who never found a public during his life, was finally driven mad with desperation and shot himself. Yet their dedication to painting never faltered, and they exemplified the French poet Baudelaire's definition of the true artist, who "is responsible to no one but himself. He donates to the centuries to come only his works; he stands surely for him-

7. *Portrait of the Artist's Son Ari,* **by Odilon Redon**

self alone. He dies without issue. He was his own king, his own priest, and his own God." What these three influential figures donated to the next generations will be clearly seen in the ensuing development of expressionism, cubism, symbolism, and various phases of abstract painting.

Matisse and the Fauves

In 1903 a group that included some young *avant-garde* painters (literally "advance guard," but loosely meaning "ahead of the times") banded together and founded the Société du Salon d'Automne[1]; their intention was to organize group exhibts where artistic freedom would be not only permitted but encouraged. Two years later, one of their showings created a major scandal in Paris. What gave offense, in particular, was one room filled with outrageous paintings by a certain Henri Matisse and his colleagues. The primary colors—red, yellow, and blue—screamed at each other from every wall. The eye was assaulted by orange fields, purple streets, and the portrait of a woman with a bright green line splitting her face. Traditional perspective had been twisted and wrenched into impossible contortions. These must be madmen! No, snickered the noted art critic Louis Vauxcelles, they are "wild beasts." Ever since, the painters of this group have been known as the Fauves (from the French for "wild beasts").

As usual the public thought it was witnessing something entirely without precedent, something entirely new that was obviously intended as a personal insult to its taste and sense of propriety. This is too often the case when the public comes face to face with a revolutionary movement in art. Ironically, these movements are rarely as revolutionary as they might at first seem. Fauvism was no exception; it had not been invented overnight. The best way to describe its gradual emergence would be to follow the career of Henri Matisse, since it was he who led the group—by example, however, rather than being their chosen leader.

Matisse was born into a respectable middle-class family at Le Cateau-Cambrésis in 1869. Following his father's wishes, he studied law. However, he suffered a serious illness at the age of twenty, and during his convalescence he took up painting, an

[1] Among the founders of the Salon were Renoir, Vuillard, Marquet, and Rouault.

activity that changed his entire life. Three years later, despite his father's protests, he entered a Parisian art school, the Académie Julien, where the students were permitted to paint and draw as they wished. Cézanne, Van Gogh, and Toulouse-Lautrec had studied there before him. The following year found him at the official art academy of Paris, the École des Beaux-Arts, where the teaching was severly disciplined and traditional. Fortunately, Matisse was able to enter the classes of Gustave Moreau, where he met such other budding masters as Georges Rouault (1871–1958) and Albert Marquet (1875–1947). Moreau, a symbolist painter best known for his jewel-toned pictures with a strong Oriental flavor, was not a progressive teacher; nevertheless, he was an excellent one, who encouraged his students to develop their own styles by studying the old masters until they knew what they wanted to take from them. This attitude suited Matisse perfectly, and he became passionately interested in such older French masters as Nicolas Poussin, Philippe de Champaigne, and Jean Baptiste Chardin, the country's greatest painter of still life in the eighteenth century. But in later years, Matisse said of this period, "The teachers at the Beaux-Arts used to say to their pupils 'copy nature stupidly.' Throughout my career I have reacted against this attitude, to which I could not submit; my struggle gave rise to various changes of course, during which I searched for means of expression beyond the literal copying—such as divisionism and Fauvism."[2]

Matisse's admiration of Cézanne's structural genius was such that he spent his wife's meager dowry on one of the older master's small pictures of bathers. Though the couple could ill afford it then, the Cézanne remained Matisse's proudest possession, and

[2] "Divisionism" refers to a theoretic method of painting invented by the neoimpressionist painter George Seurat (1859–1891). As an art historical term, "neoimpressionist" was assigned specifically to Seurat and his group. In essence, divisionism (also called "pointillism") meant the scientific breaking down of areas into tiny contrasting spots of pure color that, owing to laws of optics, blur into vibrant solid hues when seen from a distance. Seurat's technique differed from the impressionists' portrayal of flickering light in that he followed an almost purely mathematical procedure.

he later claimed that it had provided him with thirty-five years of inspiration. But it was color that appealed to Matisse more than anything else, and for a time he boldly experimented with divisionist color techniques. [Compare, for instance, Seurat's *Seine at the Grand Jatte* with Matisse's *Luxury, Peace, and Voluptuousness* (Plate 8, 9).] Matisse also learned much from the expressive, emotional color of Van Gogh and Gauguin. Gauguin's insistence on the artist's right to paint any object the color he *felt* it to be liberated Matisse further. In 1898 Matisse painted a bright blue male nude, which left even his most understanding friends speechless. He theorized that "Simple [pure] colors can act upon the inner feelings with all the more force because they are simple. A blue, for instance, accompanied by the shimmer of its complimentaries, acts upon the feelings like a sharp blow on a gong.

8. *The Seine at the Grande Jatte,* by Georges Seurat

9. ***Luxury, Peace, and Voluptuousness,*** **by Henri Matisse**

The same with red and yellow, and the artist must be able to sound them when he needs to."

Matisse was equally experimental and daring in composing a picture's overall design in relation to its edges: "The whole arrangement of my picture is expressive. The place occupied by the figures or objects, the empty spaces around them, the proportions, everything plays a part. Composition is the art of arranging in a decorative manner the various elements at the painter's disposal for the expression of his feelings."

Matisse absorbed the ideas of any and all artists who interested him, including those of the Middle East, and in this way gradually arrived at the point of realizing how his ideal painting should look. Like Cézanne, Matisse wanted to emphasize the existence of a painting as something complete in itself, with a life all its own. He wanted to create pictures that paraphrased nature rather than to copy it "stupidly," for it is impossible to reproduce nature exactly. No paint can ever be as brilliant as the most brilliant natural light. Matisse himself said, "Never struggle with nature to reproduce light; we must look for an equivalent . . . for the means we use are in themselves dead. Otherwise we would inevitably be led to place the sun behind the canvas."

Light indicates space. We would find it difficult to judge distances with any accuracy were it not for the light falling on objects as they recede toward the horizon. Matisse understood, as many artists had, that certain colors suggest space and light more than others. Warm colors (red is the strongest) appear to advance toward the viewer, and cold colors such as blues and greens to recede. Colors in the distance are more muted than those in the foreground. Why not, then, suggest light and space purely in terms of their color characteristics? All these ideas were brought together in Matisse's paintings, with his most frequent themes being figures in interior settings and still life (Plate 10). Other painters interested in these same problems were soon inspired to follow his lead.

The painters who exhibited in the original gallery of Fauves included four other ex-students of Gustave Moreau at the École des Beaux-Arts: Albert Marquet, Georges Rouault, Charles Camoin (1879–   ), and Henri Manguin (1874–1943). Matisse met Marquet, Camoin, and Manguin at school and often went sketching with them at the Louvre and in the streets of Paris. Gradually the fellow students began to paint in a similar manner. Marquet's pictures, however, show an undeniable attachment to the impressionists in his fondness for sparkling beach and street scenes. Only his bold use of pure color puts him in the general

category of the Fauves, as can be seen in the sunny spectrum of billboards in *Posters at Trouville* (Plate 11).

Manguin's experiments with using color to suggest both direct and reflected light were more adventurous than Marquet's. In

10. ***Still Life,*** **by Henri Matisse**

Woman at the Window (Plate 12), he has used a whole range of yellows, mauves, reds, and greens to give the effect of strong outdoor light falling on the shadowy figure of his model.

In 1901 this circle of friends was joined by André Derain (1880–

11. *Posters at Trouville*, by **Albert Marquet**

12. *Woman at the Window,* by Henri Manguin

13. *The Village,* by Maurice Vlaminck

14. *Westminster Bridge,* by André Derain

1954) and Maurice Vlaminck (1876–1958), who were professional athletes turned artists. They shared a studio and had developed similar painting styles. Vlaminck—bicycle racer, violinist, lover of bargemen's cafés, speed, and music halls—was born in Paris of Flemish parents. Van Gogh was his idol; in fact, Vlaminck claimed that he was more important to him than his own father. The strong influence of Van Gogh is particularly evident in *The Village* (Plate 13). Vlaminck was the soul of spontaneity, of wild expressiveness and joyous life. In these qualities he typifies most fully the spirit of Fauvism.

Derain, in turn, was influenced by Vlaminck, Matisse, Seurat, and the divisionists. The influence of the last-named can be easily detected in the treatment of sky and water in a London-inspired painting of *Westminister Bridge* (Plate 14). His colors and compositions leap with life and activity, yet are always carefully balanced. Both Vlaminck and Derain later fell under the spell of Cézanne's paintings. At this time, Vlaminck modified the brilliantly expressive daubs of color he used to portray a dancer at the notorious Paris nightclub Le Rat Mort ("The Dead Rat") for such serenely structured, more somber-colored studies as *The Old Harbor, Marseilles* (Plates 15, 16).

All these young artists banded together and exhibited at various shows around Paris, which in turn attracted new followers. The Dutchman, Kees van Dongen (1877–1968) joined them, and in 1904 their ranks were swelled by three painters from the port of Le Havre who had come under Matisse's influence: Othon Friesz (1879–1949), Raoul Dufy (1877–1953), and Georges Braque (1882–1963). Upon Matisse's suggestion, Friesz divorced himself from his original impressionist tendencies and began to study carefully the paintings of Van Gogh and Seurat, which made him realize that he "could obtain the equivalent of sunlight by a technique based on orchestrated colors and emotional transpositions of nature, and that nature yields her secrets to passionate search and enthusiasm." His own passionate search led Friesz to paint vibrant pictures full of dancing light, a fine example being his *Portrait of Fernand Fleuret* (Plate 17).

As we shall see later, Dufy's personal style was to become

15. *Dancer at "Le Rat Mort,"* **by Maurice Vlaminck**

16. ***The Old Harbor, Marseilles,*** **by Maurice Vlaminck**

extremely individual and easy to identify in the years following his association with the Fauves. A faint indication of what was to evolve can be noted in *Harbor of Le Havre* (Plate 18). The large, clearly defined areas of contrasting color (as seen in the water) would in the future serve him as flat compositional backgrounds bearing no logical relationship of form to the drawings superimposed on them. Struck by Matisse's simplified color, Dufy passed through a transitional period as a Fauve, during which he painted boldly festive scenes such as *Decorated Streets* (Plate 19).

Van Dongen's most important and unmannered work dates from the Fauve era. (It should be noted here that there was no Fauvist *period* or *school* proper; nor were the Fauves committed

17. *Portrait of Fernand Fleuret,* by Othon Friesz

18. *Harbor of Le Havre,* by Raoul Dufy

19. *Decorated Streets,* by Raoul Dufy

20. *Liverpool Nightclub,* by Kees van Dongen

21. ***Marchesa Casati,*** **by Kees van Dongen**

to any strict set of self-imposed rules or theories.) Van Dongen's Fauvism is best expressed in the exuberant color and brushstrokes of *Liverpool Nightclub* (Plate 20). Nowadays his name usually brings to mind sophisticated portraits of international beauties with bobbed hair and silent film star eye makeup. This sort of stylish picture such as his *Marchesa Casati* (Plate 21), ensured him a wide and wealthy patronage, if not permanent critical success. Nevertheless, even at their trickiest, Van Dongen's portraits retained some Fauve traits, such as the Marchesa's ultramarine blue hound.

Georges Braque's involvement with Fauvism could be called a serious "flirtation." A quiet, intelligent giant of a man, he adopted new techniques with amazing facility and understanding. His physical strength was impressive. The American avant-garde writer and art collector Gertrude Stein noted that Braque was always counted on to help hang the heaviest paintings, and that singlehandedly he had prevented two hefty statues from toppling on the guests when a banquet at Picasso's studio got out of control. It was with Picasso, too, that Braque would firmly establish his reputation as the co-developer of cubism.

With the exception of Matisse, Braque approached the art of Cézanne the most wisely. In 1908 Braque and Dufy traveled to L'Estaque, the Provençal region where Cézanne had so frequently painted. There Braque was able to see with his own eyes what had helped to inspire Cézanne's ideas concerning form and space (Plate 22). Shortly after this experience, Braque and Picasso launched their artistic revolution—a revolution which was to exceed even that of the Fauves in its consequences.

22. ***Houses at L'Estaque,*** **by Georges Braque**

Picasso and Rouault

PABLO PICASSO, the twentieth century's great innovator, was born in 1881 in Málaga, Spain, where his father, also a painter, was a teacher in the School of Arts and Crafts. During Picasso's teens the family moved to Barcelona, where his father again took up teaching. Pablo, who from childhood had given many indications of exceptional talent, entered the Barcelona Academy at the age of fifteen and pursued art studies there for several years. It has already been noted that his first actual contact with Parisian life came in 1900 at the Art Nouveau-influenced World's Fair. He was affected not only by this style but also by Toulouse-Lautrec, Gauguin, and a group called the Nabis.

The Nabis took their name from the Hebrew word meaning "prophet" or "seer." Their leader Paul Sérusier gathered this group together in Paris after returning from Brittany, where he had been closely associated with yet another group led by Gauguin at Pont-Aven. Like Gauguin, the Nabis rejected naturalism. Two of the most talented, Pierre Bonnard (1867–1947) and Edouard Vuillard (1868–1940), had a studio together and shared the same general ideas about painting. Their preferred subjects were domestic scenes composed of contrasting flat patterns and luminous color effects. Because of its intimate quality, the name "intimism" has been given to their style of painting. Bonnard was also fascinated by the idea of showing figures in silhouette, as seen in his *Dinner by Lamplight* (Plate 23). The general style of pictures like this derived from Chardin and from certain Dutch genre and still-life masters of the seventeenth century. Both Bonnard and Vuillard wished to give maximum pleasure and a comfortable satisfaction through their paintings, to create an intimate, yet colorfully expressive world (Plate 24). Among the great masters of the postimpressionist period, they continued to paint until almost the middle of the twentieth century. Bonnard, particularly, remained faithful to his early intimist ideas and style, even when dealing with subjects outside the family circle. In outdoor scenes

23. ***Dinner by Lamplight,*** **by Pierre Bonnard**

he was generally more successful in painting the small-scale landscape of gardens rather than broad expanses. He was also adept at depicting such preferred impressionist subjects as people joined in good fellowship or engaged in such pleasant pastimes as sailing (Plate 25). Mealtimes were another favorite theme (Plate 26).

Bonnard had a rare ability that was not always found in the Fauves: he could use extremely bright and vivid colors to create

a subtle instead of a harsh effect. Above all, he was able to bring a profound sense of humanity to his intimate domestic scenes.

The Flower Seller (Plate 27) was painted by Picasso in 1901, when he was twenty; in many ways it recalls a series of paintings done by Bonnard a few years earlier. By 1903 he had advanced sufficiently in his own direction to paint the overwhelming picture *Life* (Plate 28). Picasso's life-long concern for humanity domi-

24. *The Newspaper,* by Edouard Vuillard

25. *Signac and Friends Boating,* by Pierre Bonnard

26. *Dessert,* by Pierre Bonnard

27. ***The Flower Seller,*** **by Pablo Picasso**

nates this phase of his career, which is known as the "Blue Period" (roughly 1901–1904). The couple to the left in *Life* represents the values of love and marriage, while the woman and baby represent motherhood and the eternal cycles of life. The pictures on the wall portray anguish and loneliness. The paintings of the Blue period, with their predominant cool tones of blue and blue-green, usually dwell on sad or desolate people—blindmen, beggars, the hopelessly poor. These figures which are elongated, angular, and frequently as fleshless as skeletons, often sit drooping with a kind of painful grace over bleak tables (Plate 29).

The pathetic clowns that recur as themes during Picasso's Blue Period also appear in the powerful, evocative paintings of Georges Rouault. The art critic James Thrall Soby neatly summed up

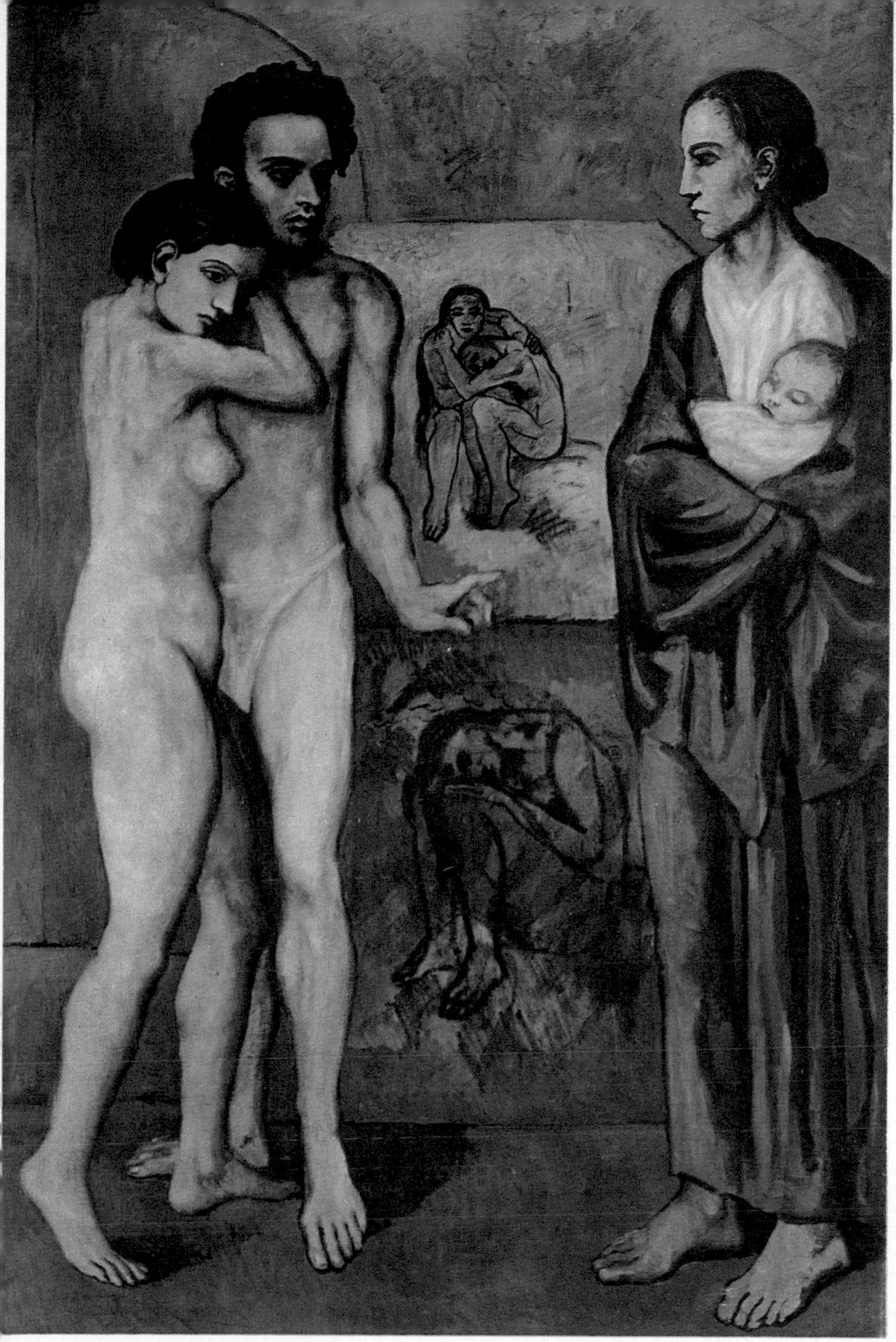

28. *Life*, by Pablo Picasso

29. *The Blindman,* by Pablo Picasso

Rouault as "a solitary figure in an era of group manifestoes and shared directions . . . an artist with a limited vision of unlimited fecundity in contrast to many other leading painters who have scanned and pivoted but seldom stared fixedly for long. . . ." Rouault, a devout Catholic, painted religious scenes at a time when this kind of subject matter had generally been abandoned by others. An emotional and moral man, he expressed his outrage at vice, hypocrisy, and corruption in rich color as brilliant as the finest stained glass. On occasion, these pictures provoked outrage on the part of their viewers which was as intense as that which had prompted their creation. Along with his stained-glass colors, the powerful black contour lines of *The Passion* (Plate 30), painted in Rouault's old age, were his trademark. It would not be stretching the point to compare Rouault's strong, structural outlines with the dark lead strips used in stained-glass windows. Therefore, it comes as no surprise to discover that Rouault had completed his apprenticeship to a stained-glass maker even before entering Gustave Moreau's studio at the Beaux-Arts in 1892. Moreau became a second father to him. Before that, his grandfather ("who loved the fine arts—but outside official circles") was his sole spiritual support. One of Rouault's earliest memories was

30. *The Passion,* by Georges Rouault

of drawing larger than life-size heads in chalk on his grandfather's polished wood floors for the old man's pleasure. His grandfather often spoke of artistic integrity and independence, and the impression these talks made went bone deep. Toward the end of his life Rouault declared, "I must say, without boasting too much about it, that I have practiced this often legendary art with more or less luck; I have respected a certain internal order and laws which I hope are traditional; removed from passing fashions and contemporaries—critics, artists, and dealers—I believe I have kept my spiritual liberty."

Picasso said that, on the whole, people looked at pictures blindly, stupidly, as they had been told to or thought they should, "instead of trying to sense what inner life there was in the men who painted them." This is a good statement to keep in mind. He added, "A picture is not thought out and settled beforehand. While it is being done it changes as one's thoughts change. And when it is finished, it still goes on changing, according to the state of mind of whoever is looking at it. A picture lives a life like a living creature, undergoing the changes imposed on us by our life from day to day. This is natural enough, as the picture lives only through the man who is looking at it."

That Picasso's thoughts were changing in 1904 becomes evident with the advent of his "Rose Period." The colors of his new paintings were predominantly pink, yellow ocher, and gray. Strolling players, acrobats, clowns, and harlequins replaced blind and destitute people as his subjects. Picasso had moved to Paris and set up a studio in Montmartre in a creaky old building nicknamed the "Bateau-Lavoir" (the French name for a clumsy boat from which laundresses used to wash clothes in the Seine). There he formed a circle of close friends including the poet, critic, and promoter of experimental art Guillaume Apollinaire and the poet Max Jacob. They made the atmosphere electric with their brilliant artistic debates. The young painter Marie Laurencin (1885–1956), who was Apollinaire's constant companion, later recalled: "The evening he [Apollinaire] usually spent at Picasso's place, 13 rue Ravignan, in company with Max Jacob and the three of them did nothing but quarrel, catch each other out, glare at each other, and, most of all, exchange curses, which was their speciality; after which they would be idolising one another all over the place."

Everyone and anyone was welcome at Picasso's table, even if there were only a couple of chairs and barely enough money to buy macaroni and mineral water. Montmartre had long been familiar with wild and uproarious Bohemians, and this new generation did nothing to let the old legends die. Near the Bateau-Lavoir were the old mills that had been converted into gay and noisily informal nightclubs, as well as a charming old-fashioned circus, whose performers Picasso idealized in his Rose period paintings (Plate 31). Picasso later dismissed this enchantingly graceful period of subtle colors and refined drawing in his career by declaring "All that was just sentiment."

In 1906, Picasso returned to Spain for the summer. There he renewed contact with Spanish Gothic sculpture and, more important, with ancient Iberian sculpture dating back to the time before the Roman Empire. Early Iberian sculpture has a stark and simple strength and unrefined, unconventional proportions, to the point of appearing primitive.

The word "primitive" has several uses and misuses in art. In one sense it can be applied to the art of primitive societies, such as tribal masks and totems. "Primitive" can also be applied to so-called "naïve" *(naif)* art, as created by self-taught artists such as Grandma Moses or Henri Rousseau (1844–1910). The Douanier Rousseau (the French *douanier* means "customs inspector"), who exhibited with the Fauves among others, because of his fantastic jungle scenes sometimes is incorrectly labeled "primitive" in both senses. His uncomplicated *Still Life* (Plate 32), painted with deceptively amateurish simplicity, clearly shows that he was a primitive of the second, self-taught category. Ironically, Rousseau's intention was never deliberately to distort but, hopefully, to paint like the great artists whose work he admired in the Louvre. We shall return to the other classification of "primitive" in our discussion of the German expressionists and of the celebrated Picasso painting that led to the development of cubism.

31. ***Family of Saltimbanques,*** **by Pablo Picasso**

32. ***Still Life,*** **by Henri Rousseau**

Under the influence of the Iberian sculpture, Picasso abandoned his Rose period and experimented in a ruggedly simplified new style, as evidenced in his *Self-portrait* (Plate 33). Such works, along with his introduction to African sculpture by Matisse, led to the revolutionary *Les Demoiselles d'Avignon* (Plate 34). This picture is essentially an arrangement of figures, but its similarity to anything ever painted before begins and ends there. The back-

33. ***Self-portrait,*** **by Pablo Picasso**

ground draperies have been flattened and violently broken up into geometric planes with a life all their own; the color, though limited in range, is peculiarly dazzling.

Les Demoiselles d'Avignon is a perfect illustration of Picasso's statement that a picture changes along with the painter's thoughts. All that remains of the original conception is the small arrangement of fruit at the bottom of the canvas. All five faces were

34. ***Les Demoiselles d'Avignon,*** **by Pablo Picasso**

at one point rendered in the Iberian-influenced style of the three on the left. The two unsettling masklike heads on the right were painted in following Picasso's sudden fascination with African primitive art. The importance of this painting was not immediately recognized by Braque, Matisse, and Derain, though none denied its harsh expressive power. It has been written about this influential work: "But it marked, none the less, the end of 500 years of tradition. A painting was no longer three-dimensional, inviting one back through a 'window' into a different world; instead space and form were manipulated by the artist on the two-dimensional picture plane. It is from such an achievement that the development of cubism proceeded."

A memorial exhibition of Cézanne in 1907 inspired Picasso to delve even deeper into the possibilities of handling formal structure and space. Cézanne's advice to treat nature in terms of the cylinder, the sphere, and the cone was adopted by Picasso not only for landscape but for still life and figures as well. By 1909–1910, he had progressed as far as the *Seated Nude* (Plate 35). This painting shows how rapidly Picasso, in the company of Braque, raced ahead of Cézanne's pioneer discoveries and opened up a whole new visual world. Realistic detail, atmospheric effects, and naturalistic color were abandoned. Attention was focused on movement in space, on seeing things from diverse angles, and on artistic means rather than on subject matter. Matisse was unmoved and contemptuously referred to these paintings as a jumble of "little cubes." The critic Louis Vauxcelles also used the word "cubist" in describing the fragmented compositions. In reply to his critics, Picasso remarked, "I paint objects as I think them, not as I see them."

Braque and Picasso spent part of the summer of 1912 together at Sorgues, near Avignon. There they took cubism a step further by introducing letters and names into their pictures. Because these were flat components, attention was drawn to the flat surface of the picture.

Braque called upon his early training as a decorator to introduce such effects as marbling, wood graining, and stencils into his paintings. Moreover, both artists began to incorporate bits and pieces of real newspaper and wallpaper into their works (Plates 36, 37). The technique of pasting cutouts onto canvas is called *papier collé;* the term "collage" was used to describe this new art medium of Braque and Picasso. Also, to distinguish the new style from their earlier one ("analytic cubism"), this phase was called "synthetic cubism."

The creation of cubism had proceeded quickly. From the summer of 1909, Braque and Picasso worked as if "roped together like mountaineers," as Braque described it. Their experiments were reaching toward a total grasp of reality, despite any apparent evidence to the contrary. Braque has said, "It was a means of getting closer to objects within the limits that painting would allow. Through fragmentation I was able to establish space and movement in space, and I was unable to introduce objects until after I had created space."

The two most important artists to adopt a cubist style of painting after 1910 were the Frenchman Fernand Léger (1881–1955) and the Spaniard Juan Gris (1887–1927). Others experimented with it with varying degrees of success and impatience, but Léger and Gris developed individual styles of enduring originality.

Léger had been trained as an architect; throughout his career he never completely lost his fascination with machinery and rather cold geometric shapes. He was yet another artist impressed by the Cézanne retrospective in 1907, and by 1910 Léger was painting cubist pictures peopled with robot-like figures, such as his *Nude Figures in a Wood* (Plate 38). By 1911 he had tilted the picture space to create greater depth and introduced bright contrasting colors into his canvases. The year 1913 saw Léger still boldly advancing in his own industrial-inspired direction. While there is no identifiable subject matter, paintings such as *Contrast of Forms* (Plate 39) suggest a violent modern mechanical activity. Léger was an intelligent man who thoughtfully expressed his feelings about the new art and its place in modern life:

> Abstract art is dominated by the same desire for complete freedom and perfection which inspires saints, heroes and madmen. It is a peak on which only a few creative artists and their admirers can maintain themselves. In fact, the very danger of this peak is the rarefied atmosphere by which he is surrounded. Modeling, contrasts, and objects disappear. All that remains are the purest and the most precise of relationships, a few colors, a few lines, some white spaces devoid of depth. Respect for the vertical plane—thin, rigid, limiting. This is the purism: incor-

35. ***Seated Nude,*** **by Pablo Picasso**

37. *The Violin,* **by Pablo Picasso**

38. *Nude Figures in a Wood,* **by Fernand Léger**

36. *Girl with a Guitar,* **by Georges Braque**

39. ***Contrast of Forms,*** **by Fernand Léger**

ruptible. The tumult and the speed of modern life, which is dynamic and full of contrasts, beat furiously against this light and brittle construction as it emerges coldly from the chaos.

Juan Gris took a cool and classical approach to cubism. This penniless little Spaniard arrived in Paris in 1906, and until 1910 he barely kept himself alive by working as a cartoonist. When he returned afterward to serious painting, he developed a disciplined and logically thought-out form of cubism, such as is seen in the severely organized and cool-colored *Still Life with Bottles and a Knife* (Plate 40). Following this phase, Gris experimented with the color and collage of synthetic cubism with truly beautiful results. In these works the contrast between reality and manipulated planes and textures provides great visual interest (Plate 41). Of this style of synthetic cubism Gris said, "I proceed from the general to the particular . . . Cézanne turns a bottle into a cylinder, but I begin with a cylinder and create . . . a particular bottle." And of Gris himself, Apollinaire wrote: "Here is the man who has meditated on everything modern, here is the painter who wants to conceive only new structures, whose aim is to draw or paint nothing but materially pure forms."

40. ***Still Life with Bottles and a Knife*, by Juan Gris**

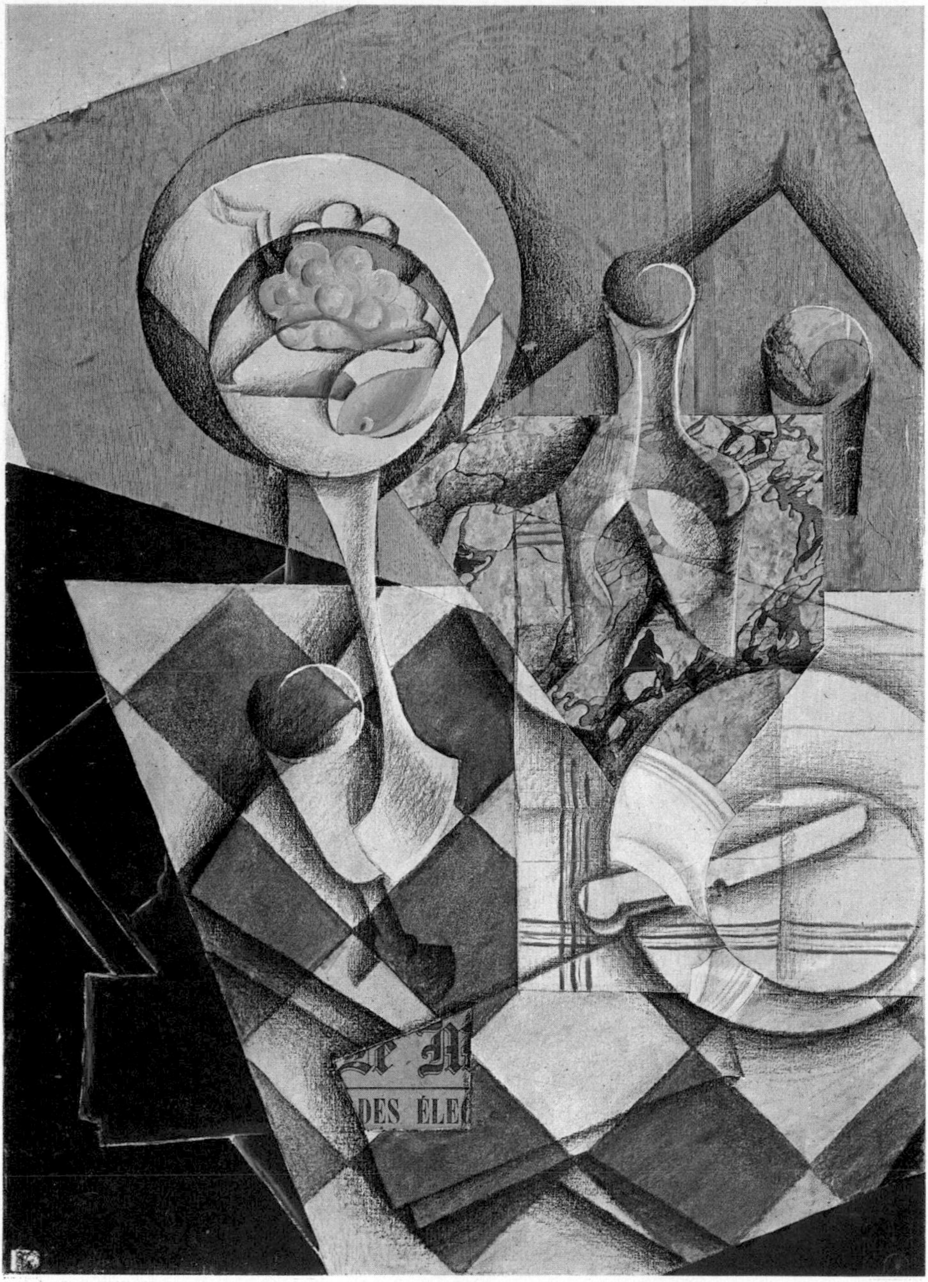

41. *Still Life with Fruit Dish and Water Bottle,* by Juan Gris

La Section d'Or

AMONG THE other, somewhat less significant followers of cubism were Albert Gleizes (1881–1953) and Jean Metzinger (1883–1956). (See Plates 42 and 43.) Together, in 1912, they published their book *Du Cubisme* ("On Cubism"), which was the first major literary piece to justify cubism. Other contemporary names of note included Robert Delaunay (1885–1941), Roger de la Fresnaye (1885–1925), Louis Marcoussis (1883–1941), and the three Duchamp brothers, who were better known individually as Jacques Villon (1875–1963), Raymond Duchamp-Villon (1876–1918), and Marcel Duchamp (1887–1968). During 1911 the work of this group was represented at three major exhibitions, and in 1912 they added the Salon de la Section d'Or ("Golden Section") to their list.

Among the Section d'Or group, led by Gaston Duchamp (under the pseudonym Jacques Villon), three important tendencies may be detected. The first was the attempt to represent movement. The second was an expanding use of color—a problem that, as you will have noticed, Picasso and Braque deliberately avoided in the early days before synthetic cubism. The third was the carrying of cubism across the threshold into the realm of purely abstract art.

The still lifes of Picasso and Braque dealt with many happy symbols of Bohemian or café life—playing cards, guitars, wine bottles, newspapers, glasses, and violins. But in 1912 a group calling themselves the futurists arrived from Italy, babbling vehemently about the glories of war, speed, power, and violent movement. Taking their cue, Villon attempted to create the effect of motion by the use of jagged patterns rather than naturalistic figures in active poses. His younger brother, Marcel Duchamp, was similarly interested in expressing movement. Duchamp's famous *Nude Descending a Staircase, No. 2* provoked a chorus of outrage when shown at the 1913 Armory Show, New York's first large-scale direct exposure to European modern art. The scandal was prompted not so much by the stated subject matter

42. *Women Sewing* by Albert Gleizes

as by the perplexing way in which it was presented. The general brownish-gold color range of *Le Passage de la Vierge à la Mariée* (Plate 44) is quite similar to that of Duchamp's more notorious work, as is its sense of progression from the upper left-hand corner to the bottom right.

Roger de la Fresnaye used bright, prettily-colored planes to add visual interest to his extremely simplified cubistic (but less fragmented) compositions, concentrating on gradations of light rather

43. ***Still Life,*** **by Jean Metzinger**

than spatial distinctions. Robert Delaunay was even more successful in drenching cubism with color. Influenced by Cézanne and early cubism, he originally painted architectural themes; but between 1910 and 1912, he gradually permitted his forms to be dissolved by light. As he wrote, "The breaking up of form by light creates colored planes. These colored planes are the structure of the picture, and nature is no longer a subject for description but a pretext." The next logical step was to abandon all attempt at

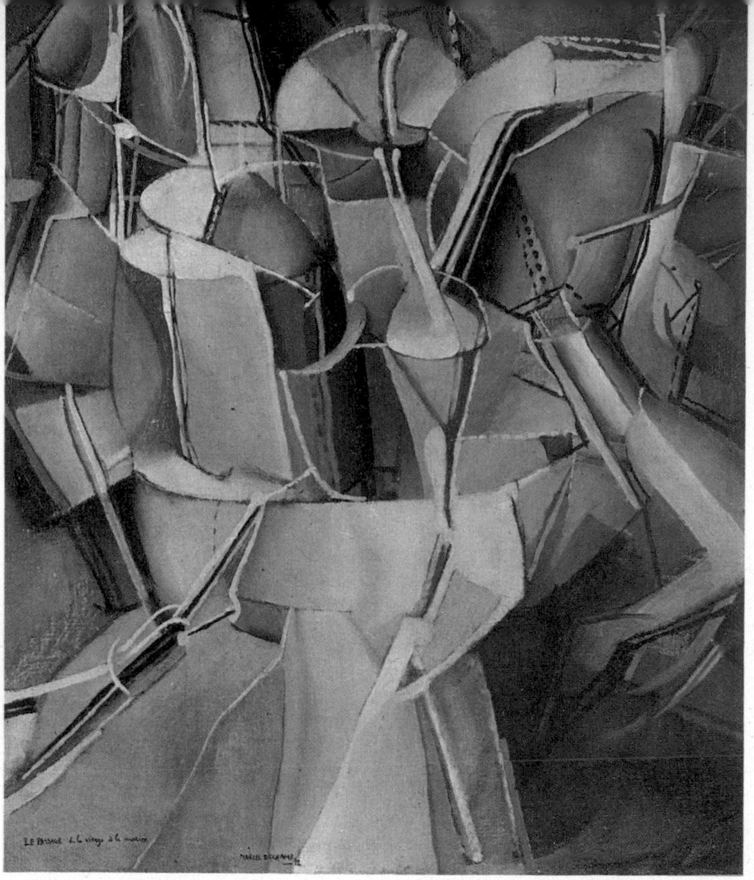

44. ***Le Passage de la Vierge à la Mariée,*** **by Marcel Duchamp**

realism and step into the colorful harmonies of pure abstract art (Plate 45).

Following in Delaunay's path was the Czech artist Frank (František) Kupka (1871–1957), who evolved an abstract art divorced from realism totally, used as a means of poetic and intellectual expression (Plate 46). Delaunay himself never went quite that far. Even at their most abstract, his paintings were meant to suggest the speed and jerky rhythms of modern life.

Cubism was initially a way of breaking down and rearranging form in terms of two, rather than three, dimensions. Nonetheless, its simplifications could be and were applied to sculpture by artists such as Henri Laurens (1885–1954), Alexander Archipenko (1887–1964), Jacques Lipchitz (1891–), Henri Gaudier-Brzeska (1891–1915), and Raymond Duchamp-Villon, and by Picasso himself.

The broken surfaces of Picasso's *Head of a Woman* (Plate 47) catch the light with a flickering effect quite like the works of Auguste Rodin, the nineteenth-century French genius who linked

45. ***Oval,*** **by Robert Delaunay**

46. ***Arrangement in Verticals,*** **by Frank Kupka**

older and modern sculpture. But Picasso has distorted and dislocated the facial structure in much the same manner as he did in his cubist paintings.

Henri Laurens' *Portrait of Marthe Girieud* (Plate 48) shows the direct influence of both cubism and the so-called "primitive" arts of Assyria. A sense of earlier primitive art is also found in the work of Alexander Archipenko. Archipenko, a Russian who was closely associated with the Salon de la Section d'Or, managed to translate cubism genuinely into sculpture by breaking his surfaces up into brightly colored geometric segments (Plate 49).

47. *Head of a Woman,* by Pablo Picasso

48. *Portrait of Marthe Girieud,* by Henri Laurens

49. ***Pierrot Carrousel,*** **by Alexander Archipenko**

The Lithuanian-born sculpture Jacques Lipchitz, about 1913–1914, "felt the necessity to bring more evident order into what nature showed me and which seemed too chaotic. . . . And I started to simplify, to abstract, to take away what did not seem essential." This desire to strip away all but the most essential distinguishing elements can be seen in his *Dancer* (Plate 50).

 Raymond Duchamp-Villon was probably the most important of

50. ***Dancer,*** **by Jacques Lipchitz**

the cubist sculptors. His work was also influenced somewhat by the Italian futurist theories of motion, as his brothers' paintings had been. In studies such as *Horse* (Plate 51), his concentration on movement has produced the simplified planes of a machine that looks as if it could uncoil dangerously at any moment. Gaudier-Brzeska, just before his death in World War I, tried to introduce this style of sculpture to England.

World War I, in which many of the cubists took part (Braque recovered from a bad wound, Apollinaire died of his), signaled the end of the style. Its effects, however, on architecture and design and on our way of looking at the world have been of lasting importance.

51. ***Horse,*** **by Raymond Duchamp-Villon**

The Futurists

THE MANNER in which Umberto Boccioni's futurist *Unique Forms of Continuity in Space* (Plate 52) is modeled bears distinct similarities to Duchamp-Villon's *Horse* (Plate 51). In this piece of sculpture Boccioni expresses the vigorous, fluid motion of a striding figure. He has said that he was attempting "to model the atmosphere that surrounds things"—a typically futurist project.

What the futurists lacked in numbers they made up for in startling declarations, noisy demonstrations, public meetings, speeches, fights, and widely publicized exhibits in all the major capitals of Europe. The movement, which was made up of young Italian artists, had been initiated by the poet and dramatist Filippo Tommaso Marinetti (1876–1944). These artists felt, with some justification, that for far too long Italy had been content with smugly resting on the laurels of its old masters. They wanted to abolish artistic dependence on the past and to set themselves up as the leaders of contemporary art. For this reason, the name "futurist" was chosen deliberately to provoke both the conservative Italian public and the progressive artists of Paris. In doing so, the Italian artists succeeded in infuriating their own countrymen, but major "French" artists such as Picasso remained aloof.

The way in which the movement was first announced was also calculated to cause a commotion. The first of the futurist manifestoes, which was concerned with literature, was published on the front page of the respectable Paris newspaper *Le Figaro,* on February 20, 1909. Written by Marinetti, it did not mince words: "We shall sing the love of danger, energy and boldness . . .," and "we declare that the world's splendor has been enriched by a new beauty, the beauty of speed. A racing motor-car, its hood adorned with great pipes like snakes with explosive breath . . . a roaring motor-car which runs like a machine gun is more beautiful than the Winged Victory of Samothrace." As if this were not sufficiently passionate or unsettling, he fanned the flames even harder: "We wish to glorify War . . . to destroy museums, the libraries."

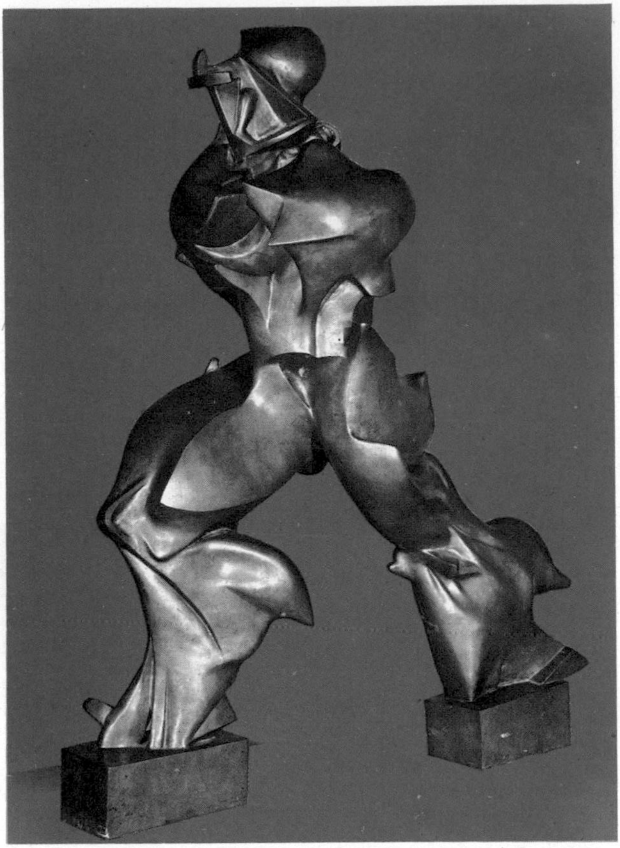

52. ***Unique Forms of Continuity in Space,*** **by Umberto Boccioni**

This was not necessarily the ranting of a madman, but a wild poetic outburst by a person who, in all truth, never really appreciated painting.

The futurist movement in Milan was joined in 1909 by three young painters, Umberto Boccioni (1882–1916), Carlo Carrá (1881–1966), and Luigi Russolo (1885–1947). They combined forces with Gino Severini (1883–1966) and Giacomo Balla (1871–1958), a teacher of both Boccioni and Severini. Together they produced the technical manifesto *La pittura futurista* ("Futurist Painting"), which, before its publication on April 11, 1910, was proclaimed from a theater stage in Turin.

Their arguments were presented logically. First, they stated flatly that their growing need for truth could no longer be satisfied with form and color as these had been understood in the past. Artists should strive to represent dynamic movement and speed by the breaking down of forms and shapes. Like the cubists, they felt that space was the atmosphere around figures and therefore should be given equal attention in painting. But, in theory they went further and insisted that all movement around, as well as space near and far, must be studied as part of what they labeled "universal dynamism." They wanted to "put the spectator in the center of the picture" by realizing the theory that "movement and light destroy the materiality of bodies." Other less important, yet refreshingly unusual ideas included: "Art critics are useless or harmful"; "The name of 'madman' with which it is attempted to gag all innovators should be looked upon as a title of honor"; and finally, "We demand, for ten years, the total suppression of the nude in painting." Their convictions seem particularly outspoken when one learns that, still no paintings had been produced to put these theories into practice.

Of the five painters who had signed the manifesto, Balla, who was exploring the divisionist style in Rome, was perhaps the most established artist. Severini, on the other hand, had lived in Paris since 1906, knew Picasso and Braque, and was well aware of all the latest French artistic developments. He had been using a complicated divisionist technique derived from Seurat's paintings. Both Carrà and Boccioni had painted sentimental pictures in which symbolist influence could be noticed. However, just before the birth of futurism, Boccioni switched styles and adapted divisionism to his gloomy realistic pictures. Russolo, who had received a thorough musical training, was later to become involved as a composer with futurist "noise machines." His painting was essentially self-taught. Each of these painters worked toward his own conception and interpretation of futurism for their first group exhibition in April, 1911.

Boccioni's first notable futurist picture was *The Riot in the Galleria* (Plate 53). At first glance, he seems primarily interested in depicting a fight between two women in front of a café. The artist's real intention was to express the effect of a surging, hysterical crowd that streams toward the center of the picture, in contrast to the stable vertical lines of the buildings. His divisionist handling of color heightens the feeling of movement and sparkling light. Nevertheless, the spectator has not been put "in the center of the picture" as the manifesto demanded he should. One sees the action as he would in a still photograph outside a movie house; one does not feel involved in the violence.

53. *The Riot in the Galleria,* by Umberto Boccioni

Boccioni's next major work succeeded more fully in conveying futurist ideals. Before painting it he had said, "I feel I want to paint the new . . . I am nauseated by old walls and old palaces. I want the new, the expressive, the wonderous and wonderful." He found this in the vast construction projects then being undertaken in the suburbs of Milan. He was particularly excited by the huge straining workhorses as appropriate symbols of the new construction. In a series of sketches for the finished picture, which was entitled *The City Rises,* he "tried for a great synthesis of labor, light and movement," using slashes of bright color in a modified divisionist manner to convey a feeling of strenuous activity and surging energy. Meanwhile, with some success, Carrà had also attempted to paint a picture of action and violence. His subject was the funeral of the anarchist Galli, an event that had taken place in 1904.

When these pictures were finally exhibited, the reaction was hardly what the artists had hoped for. The Italian painter and critic Ardengo Soffici (1879–1964) wrote an article for *La Voce,* published in Florence, in which he took the exhibitors to task for their ignorance of contemporary developments. Severini returned from Paris and was equally horrified at their backwardness. Boccioni and Soffici fell into a fistfight; and since Soffici immediately afterward took up the futurist cause, someone clearly must have proved a point.

Severini's criticisms could not be so readily dismissed, and Boccioni, Carrà, and Marinetti soon made a hasty trip to Paris to catch up on the latest works at the Salon d'Automne. The trip was a fruitful one. Upon his return, Boccioni drastically altered a series of paintings he had already begun. These were called *States of Mind* (I, "The Farewells"; II, "Those Who Go"; III, "Those Who Stay"). In them, a new and more complicated cubist conception of space was combined with the emotional expression of states of mind—for Parisian painters were not interested in states of mind. The mood of *States of Mind II* is established by sweeping diagonal planes, repeated forms, and overall bluish tones. The effect is of people moving quickly away, and the spectator becomes involved and senses their hurried departures and numb

54. ***What the Tram Said to Me,*** **by Carlo Carrà**

sadness. This sort of emotional effect is at odds with the cool formal arrangements of analytical cubism.

Carrà also produced a painting in which contemporary life is expressed through a modern style—*What the Tram Said to Me* (Plate 54). Here all the noise and bustle of a crowded city street is brought to life through jagged forms, flashing lights, and shifting shadows.

These arresting works created a sensation when exhibited in Paris in February, 1912. Marinetti publicized them in his typical aggressive fashion and increased the uproar. The champion of cubism, Apollinaire, took great pride in sensitivity to changing artistic winds. Accordingly, he had to begrudge the futurists some praise for their concern with modern life, its vitality and movement. The exhibition then toured Europe for a year. Futurism had arrived as an international style; but like many modern styles, its initial phase was to last only until the eve of World War I.

Between 1912 and 1914, the futurist artists dependently expanded their personal styles. Only the magazine *Lacerba,* which was committed to the cause of futurism, continued to recognize a common bond between their styles. Severini, for example, had

55. ***Dancer in Blue,*** **by Gino Severini**

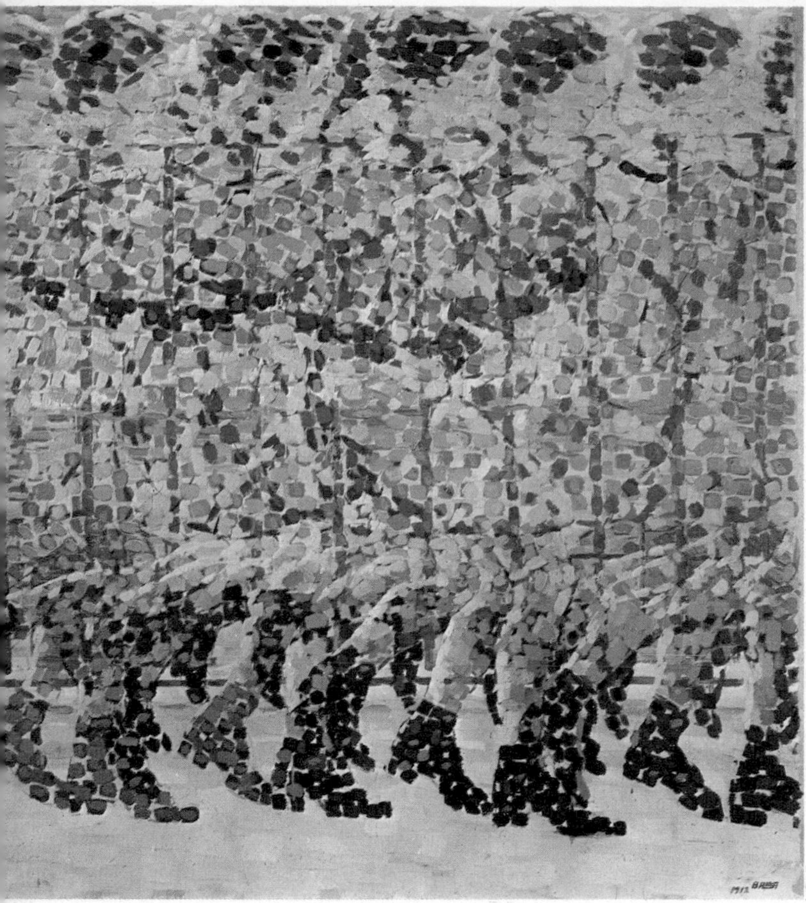

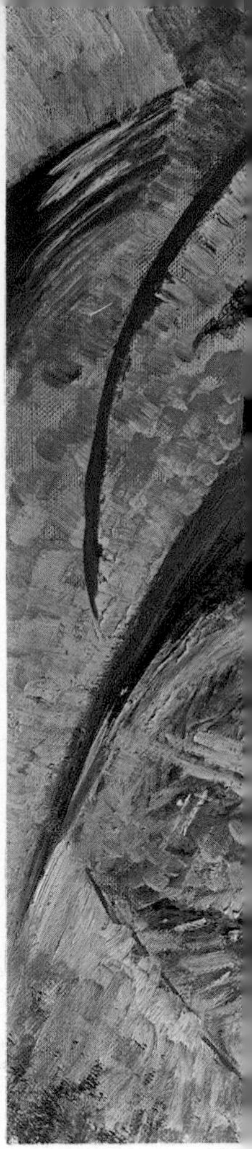

56. ***Little Girl Running on the Balcony,*** **by Giacomo Balla**

always been closer to Parisian trends. His *Dancer in Blue* (Plate 55) is basically a cubist painting put into motion. The bright color and the forms suggested by curves, rather than angles, differ somewhat from analytical cubist works. The trick of pasting sequins on the canvas, however, is borrowed directly from them.

Balla, on the other hand, remained in Rome to develop his own style of futurism, founded on a divisionist theory of color. Series of simultaneous photographs of figures in motion had deeply impressed him, *Little Girl Running on the Balcony* (Plate 56) shows

57. *Dynamism of a Cyclist,* by Umberto Boccioni

how he synthesized these photographic effects and divisionist spots of color.

Along with his sculptural experimentation, Boccioni extended his theories of dynamism and painted the explosive *Dynamism of a Cyclist* (Plate 57). This picture is almost a pure abstract and resembles somewhat the works of Kandinsky, a pioneer in modern art whom we shall study shortly. Boccioni, ironically, was killed in a riding accident in 1916 while on leave to recover from war wounds.

59. *Patriotic Celebration,* by Carlo Carrà

58. *Pursuit,* by Carlo Carrà

The futurists had idealized war as "the only health-giver in the world"; hence such pictures as Carrà's *Pursuit* (Plate 58). The random letters at the left in *Pursuit* commemorate a French victory by Marshal Joffre. The patriotism of the futurists was unbridled, as can be seen in Carrà's abstract creation *Patriotic Celebration* (Plate 59). The slogan "VI(II)VA(AA) IL RE(EE)" ("Long live the king!") spins wildly around the center, as the sounds of motors ("TRRRR, BRRRR, traak tatatraak") rumble and bounce about the edges. Names of various newspapers and journals, such as the futurist *Lacerba,* and words alluding to modern urban life and entertainment ("street," "noises," "sports," "music," "songs") are scattered across the surface. The title of the work is perhaps reflected in the repetition of "Italy" and "Italian" at several spots throughout the canvas.

Because of pictures like these, the world began henceforth to associate modern art with revolution and violence. Ironically, the war that so thrilled the futurists brought an end to their ideals, for afterward the survivors went on to paint in another style.

Die Brücke and the Viennese School

IN 1905 a circle of restless young German artists founded a revolutionary group called Die Brucke ("The Bridge"). Led by Ernst Ludwig Kirchner (1880–1938), this group included Erich Heckel (1883–   ), Karl Schmidt-Rottluff (1884–   ), and Fritz Bleyl (1880–   ). They were all architectural students, and only Kirchner had received any formal art training. They detested the cruel social caste system of Germany, especially the way in which the lower classes were suppressed both economically and educationally; yet they had no sympathy for ignorance. Their motto was "Odi profanum vulgus" ("I hate the uninitiated common masses"), and they denounced the stodgy "Victorian" German society for permitting conditions to continue as they were. German expressionism was born of this crying need for change.

Die Brücke believed fanatically in the constructive joys and ideas of group activity. Everything should be accomplished together, with mutual enthusiasm. The only drawback to this theory was that, while sounding the signal to plunge ahead, it left little time for individual reflection, logic, or order.

Together the members of the group took over a former cobbler's workshop in a working-class district of Dresden. Together they built furniture, carved stools, and put canvases around the walls of the group's new home and studio. Together they began to take drawing lessons from Fritz Schumacher (1869–1957), a distinguished town planner and architect who taught at the Dresden Academy of Art. Schumacher had impressed on them the need for unity and for personal expression. Among outsiders, he alone suspected the true quality of the group. "In my horror at the messy drawings of those students," he remembered much later, "I could not pretend to understand the young ducklings who swam away from me, unexperienced mother hen that I was. But if I remained doubtful for the time being about the artistic value, I had on the other hand a definite feeling for the human value."

The group insisted that "art depends on inspiration, not on technique." Meanwhile, Sigmund Freud's radical ideas on psychoanalysis and the subconscious were being published; and in music Arnold Schönberg's revolutionary scale system defied and openly broke with the harmonic laws of the past. The old conservative, safe and orderly life was starting to crumble. Die Brücke looked for inspiration in everything not associated with academic culture. Kirchner reintroduced the woodcut, with its primitive strength and energy, from its native southern Germany. Heckel revived wood carvings, and Kirchner colored them. Schmidt-Rottluff made the first lithographs directly on stone. Together the group "discovered" African Negro art and idolized Van Gogh, Gauguin, and Munch.

It should be remembered that Die Brücke's development came at more or less the same time as that of the Fauves; yet the sources from which they drew inspiration clearly distinguished them from the Fauves. The violent, anguished use of color by Van Gogh and Gauguin was extremely personal and at times exotic. Some of the "primitive" elements in their art could indeed be found in the work of Derain, Vlaminck, and Picasso; nevertheless, it would seem that the Germans arrived at their bold style independently. Die Brücke had also been influenced by their studies of native art from Africa and the South Pacific in the Dresden Museum of Ethnography. They also learned much about the use of symbolic color from Signac and were moved by the sorrow and melancholy of Munch's paintings.

It must be emphasized that, though their art had vague links with Africa and the South Seas, these young artists were thoroughly German or "Northern" in outlook. The barbaric savagery of some of their paintings may disguise a basic severity and starkness that harks back to the age of the Teutonic barbarians. Northern artists and writers have frequently explored dark and neurotic themes of decadence and torment. Their preoccupation has been with the troubled human condition. Such Northern attitudes, therefore, should be expected to show themselves in the expressionism of Die Brücke. Furthermore, working together in

60. ***Self-portrait with a Model,*** **by Ernst Ludwig Kirchner**

this communal spirit was thought to be a Northern idea, with roots in the medieval guild system.

Like the futurists, the Brucke group vigorously rejected all academic conventions. Cubism was an art of calm analysis; Die Brücke's was one of highly imaginative personal and emotional expression. Above anyone or anything else, Van Gogh had the greatest single influence on the German group's ideas.

Kirchner's intellectual ability and his preoccupation with theory automatically made him the group's leader. His *Self-portrait with a Model* (Plate 60) sets the style of their work. The viewer is immediately struck by the violently contrasting primary colors, the bold play of horizontal stripes and flat patterns, the masklike faces, and the dominating character of the artist. Color is used expressively rather than to define space or model the forms. In other paintings by Kirchner, faces and figures are more grotesque than in the self-portrait; they are influenced both by Gothic woodcuts and by Picasso's African-inspired heads. Kirchner never painted totally abstract compositions, because his emotional involvement with reality was too great.

The Brücke artists worked in Dresden during the winter and by the North Sea in the summer. It was there, by the sea, that they began painting boldly simplified landscapes in bright colors. Schmidt-Rottluff, in his *Forest* (Plate 61), created artificial but

61. *Forest,* by Karl Schmidt-Rottluff

62. ***Two Men Seated at a Table,*** **by Erich Heckel**

vibrant arrangements of red and blue tree trunks singing out against green, orange, and blue. He followed Gauguin's method of using unnatural and imaginative color and between 1907 and 1913 painted landscapes regularly every summer.

Heckel's particular enthusiasms were for "the visions of Van Gogh and Munch"; he also admired primitive art. A synthesis of these two interests can be seen in such paintings as *Two Men Seated at a Table* (Plate 62). We are presented with an extremely sinister, even frightening scene. The faces are again masklike in a primitive manner, but are highly expressive. One wonders what terrible thing is about to take place. Is the man on the right about to sit, or is he rising to knife the other? Have others just left them to themselves, or are the empty chairs for new arrivals? The agonized image of Christ on the wall heightens the morbid atmosphere; the portrait of a man with downcast eyes on another wall of the room seems to understand the secret but will tell us nothing.

In 1910 Otto Müller (1874–1930) joined the Brücke group. For Müller, who was a descendant of gypsies, pictures of innocent figures set in dreamlike landscapes were an obsession. As a reac-

63. ***Children in a Wood,*** **by Otto Müller**

tion against the modern mechanized world, he created a never-never land of gypsies and naked children in natural surroundings (Plate 63). This sort of idyllic world was like that which Gauguin had brought to life in his Tahitian canvases. Müller's sadly nostalgic images stand somewhat apart from the torment of the rest of the Brücke group, but his elfin figures remain expressive symbols of his contempt for "civilized" cities, a contempt shared by all the Brücke members.

In 1906 the group persuaded Emil Nolde (1867–1956) to join them, but he was to remain a member for only fifteen months. Nolde always stood somewhat outside the group. He had been painting longer than the others and had developed his own private vision. Though his style was similar to that of the Brücke artists, he remained "the great solitary of German expressionism." Earlier in his career he had painted naturalistically, but with a Northern sense of strange grimness. In 1905 he abruptly changed his style after being introduced to the paintings of Van Gogh. This influence can be seen in a series of garden paintings executed in 1907–1908 (Plate 64). His interest in primitive art was extended by

64. ***Garden with Red and Yellow Roses,*** **by Emil Nolde**

a trip to the Pacific islands in 1913–1914. He quickly adopted the "stylized, rhythmical and decorative" qualities of Pacific native art in his own work. Probably more clearly than any other painter who was influenced by primitive art, Nolde was able to answer the question "Why is it that we artists are so entranced by the primitive expression of the savages? . . . With the material in his hand, between his fingers, the artist creates his work. The expressed purpose is desire for and love of creation. The absolute originality, the intense, frequently grotesque expression of strength and life in the simplest form—that could be the factor which gives us so much joy."

In Nolde's *Dancers* (Plate 65), we see him applying this primitive "expression of strength and life in the simplest form" to his own art. The beautiful, strong colors are handled masterfully. Nolde felt deeply about color, and he might have been speaking for all fellow artists who have been emotionally moved by color when, most poetically, he expressed his feelings this way: "Colors, the materials of the painter; colors in their own lives, weeping and laughing, dream and bliss, hot and sacred, like love songs . . . like songs and glorious chorales! Colors in vibration, pealing like silver bells and clanging like bronze bells, proclaiming happiness, passion and love, soul, blood and death."

The Brücke group moved to Berlin in 1910. This move marked the beginning of the gradual breakup of the group. Later, in 1913, Kirchner wrote a history of the association, which the other members considered a highly displeasing distortion of the facts. This unfortunate incident caused the final disintegration of the once inseparable artistic circle.

The feeling of unrest that drove the artists to new ideas in Dresden, Paris, and Milan was evident also in Vienna, but in a slightly different way. "Jugendstil," the German variant of Art

65. *Dancers*, by Emil Nolde

Nouveau, had been so called after the magazine *Jugend* ("Youth"), first published in 1896. The style, in which a sinuous and decorative line was the essential element, was practically interchangeable with its French and English counterparts. The Brücke group washed their hands of it in contempt. In Vienna, however, two important painters, Egon Schiele (1890–1918) and Oskar Kokoschka (1886–), gave a last twist to Jugendstil. In contrast to the angular harshness of the Brücke painters, Schiele developed a lovely manner in which he put coiling line through the most dramatic contortions. Schiele's paintings are brightly colored and intricately patterned, and his drawing is superb, as is seen in the *Portrait of Edith, the Artist's Wife* (Plate 66).

Some authorities claim that Kokoschka's style derived from the decorative tendencies of Jugendstil. There may be some truth in this, but Kokoschka himself has said that the strongest influence during his youth was Austrian baroque art, particularly the elaborate ceiling and wall paintings in the churches of that period. In 1904, at the age of eighteen, Kokoschka entered the Vienna School of Arts and Crafts; and in 1908 he held his first exhibition as a painter. His creative energy was too great to channel into just one area of artistic activity; he also wrote plays, illustrated books, sculpted, and designed posters and decorative panels. Outstanding among his early works are a series of portraits done in 1909–1910. These are penetrating and dramatic character studies. What made them expressionistic was Kokoschka's feverish search for the soul of his subject and the exaggerated linear style he used in achieving this. A fine example of these expressionistic studies is the *Portrait of Professor Auguste Farel* (Plate 67); the sitter was a famous zoologist who lived in Switzerland. The subdued color is relatively unimportant, for it is the expressionistic drawing of the face and hands that commands our attention.

Kokoschka's talent was recognized by Herwarth Walden (1878–), the writer, gallery owner, and publisher of the influential magazine *Der Sturm* and the Viennese artist was encouraged to move to Berlin in 1910. From then onward, he played an important role in the development of German expressionism. Kokoschka's style grew much freer in its drawing and in the use of thicker.

66. *Portrait of Edith, the Artist's Wife,* by Egon Schiele

brighter pigments in later works such as *The Heathen* (Plate 68). He remained a dominant figure in European painting for decades, much admired for his personal and imaginative transformation of reality.

68. ***The Heathen,*** **by Oskar Kokoschka**

67. ***Portrait of Professor Auguste Farel,*** **by Oskar Kokoschka**

Development of Abstract Art: Blaue Reiter and De Stijl

THE TYPICAL CONTEMPORARY lack of concern with natural appearances in art is due entirely to the experiments of such artists as Kupka, Delaunay, Kandinsky, Mondrian, and Malevich. These pioneers of abstract painting stressed the relationship between abstract art and music, for they considered both as pure art forms. They began to think of art as, fundamentally, the arrangement of lines, shapes, and colors on a flat surface. These arrangements were intended to give pleasure through their own harmonies, and reference to the outside world or identifiable subject matter was no longer necessary.

Before these new trends emerged, the impressionists had developed an almost perfect technique for representing the natural world. Photography, which was rapidly gaining in use, now offered the ultimate in accuracy for recording outward appearances. In reaction, artists turned inward to their private worlds. Some, like Kandinsky in his earliest phase, turned to a free development of color in which natural objects were gradually dissolved in a mysterious world of expressive paint. Others such as Mondrian and Malevich evolved a world of pure geometry from their earlier experiments with cubism. Kandinsky eventually followed them into this last particular world of pure abstraction, where emotion is aroused by severe arrangements of basic forms and manipulation of color. Yet there continued the long-standing opposition between the intellectual and the emotional approaches to art, as will be seen below.

At the beginning of the twentieth century, Munich provided a healthy artistic climate in which to experiment. The dominant style was still Jugendstil, but the Munich artists were conscious of developments in Paris and elsewhere. The arrival of Wassily Kandinsky (1866–1944), a Russian, was to prove extremely important for Munich's artistic life. Kandinsky came to art late, at the age of thirty. His earliest ambition was to become a musician —which is interesting in that, later, he so frequently associated painting with music. Initially, Kandinsky had entered Moscow University in 1886 to study law and economics. There he first came into contact with the rich, unearthly glow of traditional Russian art and medieval icons (holy images); these works made a profound impression on him and greatly influenced his artistic development. Kandinsky also studied Russian folk art and was enchanted by its riotous colors.

In 1895, two years after receiving his law degree, Kandinsky was exposed for the first time to the paintings of the French impressionists. Immediately his mind was made up; he gave up his legal career and took off for Munich, where he enrolled at the Royal Academy. After three years of classes, he began to work independently. Between 1903 and 1908 he traveled widely in France, Tunisia, and Italy, but kept in close touch with developments in Paris all the while. Later he wrote, "Matisse—color. Picasso—form. Two great signposts pointing towards a great end."

Kandinsky's early art, though colorful and free, was not really very close to Fauvism. At first his art had been more influenced by his Russian background, a tendency that was not surprising in the grandson of an Asiatic princess. He became increasingly obsessed with this mysterious world of color in which objects seemed to dissolve. It took him some time to re-create it in his paintings. Gradually he turned away from the copying of actual appearances, saying, "I sometimes paint a landscape from memory better than after nature." For a while he painted historical pictures, with the color laid on in flat patches like a decorative tapestry. *Crinolines* (Plate 69), for example, with its flattened figures in historical costume, reminds us that Kandinsky wished to create an art of the imagination. The rough brushwork, however, was boldly modern in spirit.

Kandinsky was aware of developments in Dresden, in particular of the Brücke group. His concern with the "mystery" of painting gradually led him away from using recognizable figures and objects; but, he asked himself, "What should replace the missing object?" He was afraid of falling into a style in which the final

effect would be no more than decorative or ornamental. Consequently, he dedicated himself to the idea of "inner necessity," feeling that "as musical sound acts directly on the soul, so do form and color." The major step between reference to visual reality and the creation of an image completely independent of reality can be seen in *Paradise* and *With the Black Arch* (Plates 70, 71). In the first-mentioned picture, houses and landscape can still be identified amid the flurry of brushstrokes; in the second, the visionary effect of a landscape as if in motion is made without naturalistic features. Its logic is its own "inner necessity." Through its mysterious colorful world Kandinsky attempts to approach a

69. ***Crinolines,*** **by Vassily Kandinsky**

universal truth—a central being at the heart of all things. He felt he would be unable to express this by traditional methods of painting. "To spell out the mysterious through the mysterious—is that not content?" he wrote in 1910. In essence, Kandinsky had created abstract art.

Kandinsky was a skillful organizer as well as a great spiritual and theoretical force. In 1909 he had founded the New Artists' Association in Munich, which by 1911 had already begun to affect the cultural life of the city. At this time, however, the association split in two. The backward-looking artists considered Kandinsky's new theories of abstract art too dangerous in their implications;

70. *Paradise,* by Vassily Kandinsky

a quarrel arose over the exhibition of one of his paintings. Kandinsky, with a few friends, including the young Franz Marc (1880–1916), withdrew from the group. Around Maria Marc's tea table, they created a new group—the Blaue Reiter (its name being taken from one of Kandinsky's pictures, *The Blue Rider,* which was also to be the name of the art magazine they planned to publish).

This progressive group opened an exhibit of its own in the same gallery a few weeks afterward. The artists represented were Kandinsky and Marc, Gabriele Munter (1877–1962), August

Macke (1887–1914), Heinrich Campendonk (1889–1957), the two Russians David (1882–1967) and Vladimir (18??–19) Burliuk. and the avant-garde composer Arnold Schonberg (1874–1951), who was also a painter. Kandinsky included two French painters whom he considered important as examples of opposite extremes: Robert Delaunay and Henri Rousseau. By 1912 the Russian Alexei von Jawlensky (1867–1941), as well as Alfred Kubin (1877–1959) and the Swiss Paul Klee (1879–1940), had also joined the Blaue Reiter circle. Touring exhibitions that were arranged by the group showed examples of the various abstract tendencies of the times.

August Macke, though equally involved with the Blaue Reiter group, developed along different lines. Concerning himself very much with color, he was also impressed by cubist simplification and the art of Rousseau. Though interested in representing states of mind and abstract theories, Macke never painted wholly abstract pictures. Influenced by a simple type of cubism, he created doll-like figures that exist in an airless world of their own (Plate 72). Macke, too, was killed early in World War I.

Alexei von Jawlensky was an army officer before he went to study art in Munich. Between 1902 and 1910, he traveled widely and was much affected by the paintings of Matisse and the Fauves that he encountered. Before the outbreak of the war he produced a series of large, powerfully colored heads and simplified figures. *The White Plume* (Plate 74) shows how he was developing toward this style; the figure fills the picture area, and the paint is thick and colorful. In later paintings, his outlines became deliberately more crude and primitive. Although he never became completely an abstract artist, he shared a spiritual bond with his Munich associates. His freely painted works, which owe much to the example of Gauguin and Matisse, remain expressive and symbolic images (Plate 73).

Germany, and in particular Munich, had been the natural place to study for many Russian artists. They did not, however, neglect Paris. From 1906 onward, Diaghilev's Russian ballet company and its designers created an enormous stir in Paris. Serge Diaghilev (1872–1929) conceived a ballet in which music, dancing, decor (set

71. ***With the Black Arch,*** **by Vassily Kandinsky**

decoration), and costumes all formed a single brilliantly unified whole. Soloists, no matter how distinguished, formed part of that unity, as did every member of the chorus. In décor and costumes he also broke new ground by commissioning designs from well-known artists. In the past, ballet décor had all too frequently been limited to a misty, vaguely romantic backdrop containing a forest or a lake. Through such commissions a new integration of costumes and settings was achieved. Some art movements such as rayonism, developed by Larionov and Gontcharova, found their fullest expression in the theater. Between 1911 and 1914, Mikhail Larionov (1881–1964) and his wife Natalia Gontcharova (1881–1962), Russian artists who exhibited at the second Blaue Reiter show in 1912, launched a style to which they gave the dismaying name "rayonism." Influenced by cubism and futurism, this style was characterized by luminous rays that its creators called "lines of force."

Later, Diaghilev was forced to turn more and more to Western Europe for inspiration. As always, he sought the finest artists, so that eventually Picasso, Matisse, Griss, Braque, Derain, Rouault, and others were all enlisted to contribute their creative genius to his Ballet Russe productions.

Another significant Russian painter, Kazimir Malevich (1878–1935), founded a new movement that he called "suprematism." Malevich had run through a whole gamut of Western European styles, ending with cubism, but none seemed to suit him for long. Disenchanted, he proceeded to create a completely abstract art based on the simplest geometric forms. His first suprematist picture was a black square on a white background. Nothing could be simpler. The two contrasting colors he considered the basis of all art, and he felt that "reality in art was the sensational effect of color itself." His position was later explained by members of a progressive school called the Bauhaus:

> The representation of an object, in itself . . . is something that has nothing to do with art, although the use of representation in a work of art does not rule out the possibility of its being of a high artistic order. For the suprematist, therefore, the proper means is the one that provides the fullest expression of pure feeling and ignores the habitually accepted object. The object in itself is meaningless to him; and the ideas of the conscious mind are worthless. Feeling is the decisive factor . . . and *thus art arrives at non-objective representation*—at suprematism.

Eight Red Rectangles, for example, presents its own language of form. Malevich expected that his pure art form should, like music, be understood without reference to the world of appearances. The development of this abstract style was important in Russia and elsewhere for its new approach to basic design principles in the applied arts and architecture.

Painters in Holland who were aware of contemporary developments in France started the group known as De Stijl ("The Style"). Holland produced an equally spare and harmonious art based on

72. *Separation,* by August Macke

73. *Still Life,* by Alexei von Jawlensky

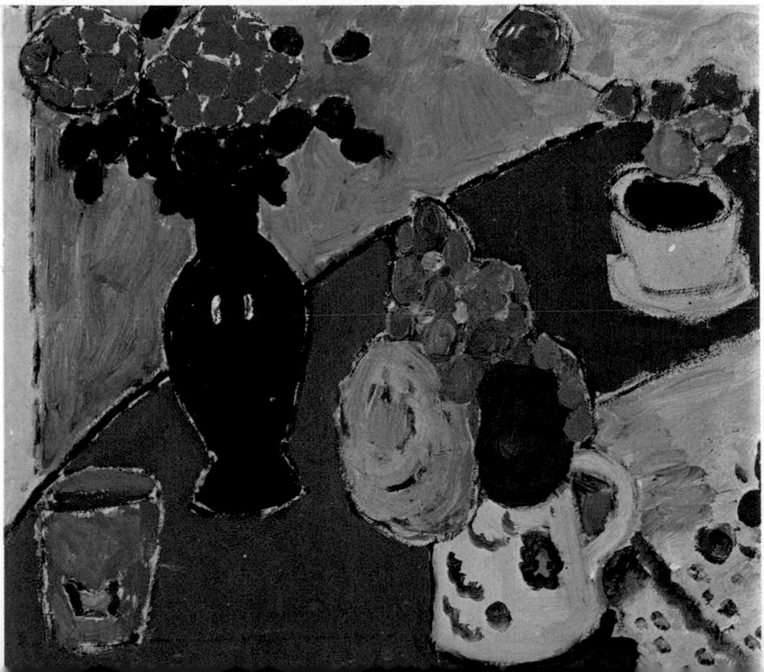

74. *The White Plume,* by Alexei von Jawlensky

the same fundamentals that Malevich had applied in evolving suprematism in Russia. The De Stijl group was made up of artists and designers whose achievements soon affected both modern architecture and interior design. The revolution they caused in typography (the art of printing with type, which involves design of lettering styles, or typefaces, and effective page layouts) and advertising layout is still apparent today. Its Dutch origins very likely gave this new art form its logic, simplicity, and severe, orderly structure. Fancy brushwork or extravagant personal mannerisms were not to be tolerated.

Piet Mondrian (1872–1944), De Stijl's greatest genius, remained true to his own early artistic concepts during the whole of his career. Having begun to draw and paint while very young in his village home, he left his teaching studies in order to begin formal art training in Amsterdam. He painted in a rather impressionist manner until 1911, when he went to Paris. There he quickly became an admirer of the cubist paintings of Picasso and Léger.

The important early phase of his career occurred between 1911 and 1916, when he sought to abstract the basic lines and harmonies of trees, still lifes, and seascapes. The recognizable abstracted forms became simpler and simpler, much as they had in the paintings of Kandinsky; but there was a major difference. Kandinsky had sought in nature the mystery and suggestion of color. Mondrian was searching for the underlying lines of balance in nature. At first glance, *Composition in Line and Color* (Plate 75), dating from 1912–1913, suggests a cubist still life, but the objects have been turned into a series of vertical and horizontal lines broken by an occasional arc. The color range of yellow ochers and grays is typically cubist.

When World War I broke out in 1914, Mondrian was in Holland, which remained a neutral country. Unable to return to Paris, he spent his time on a series of pictures based on the sea waves and breakwaters at Domburg. Composed of crisscrossed and short horizontal lines, these have been called Mondrian's "plus-minus" works. The rhythm of the waves rolling into shore is expressed by short horizontal strokes that gradually spread toward the bottom of the picture. Although these pictures appear to be purely ab-

75. ***Composition in Line and Color,*** **by Piet Mondrian**

stract, Mondrian resented their minimal reference to nature. "The emotion of beauty is always obstructed by the appearance of the 'object'; therefore the object must be eliminated from the picture."

Mondrian had reached this important conclusion in 1915, the momentous year when he met Theo van Doesburg (1883–1931), (Plate 76) the nervously brilliant critic, painter, architect, and poet. The following year he became acquainted with Bart van der Leck (1876–1958), who had produced abstract pictures composed

77. ***Geometric Composition II,*** **by Bart van der Leck**

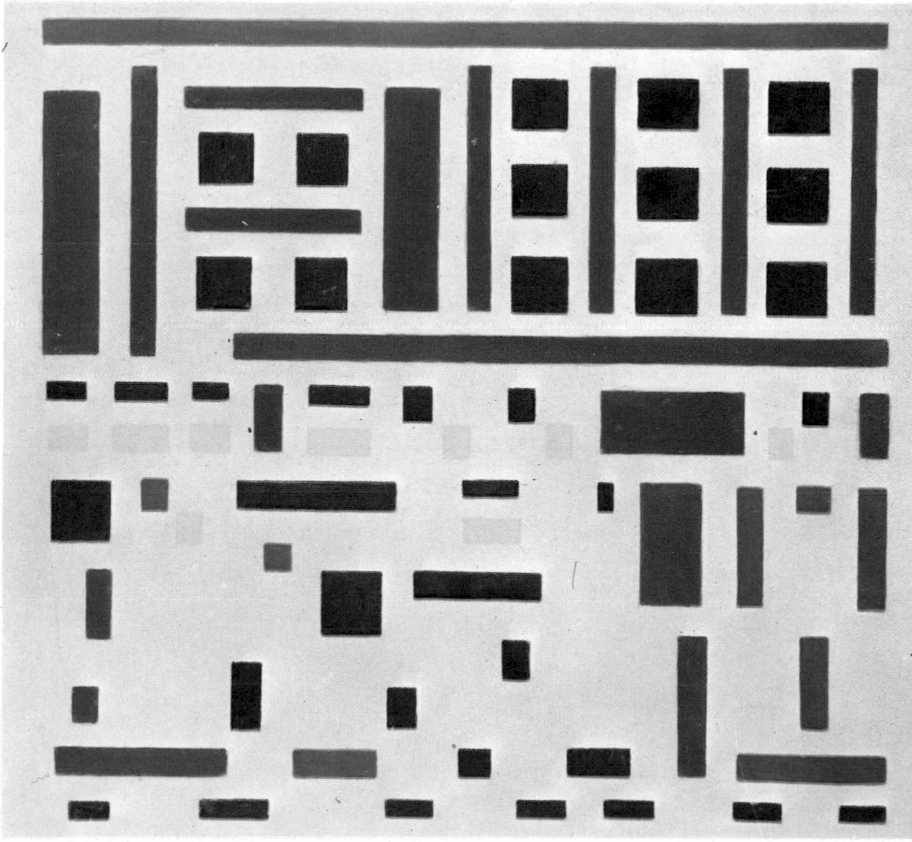

76. ***Geometric Composition,*** **by Theo van Doesburg**

of simple rectangles in black and the primary colors of red, yellow, and blue (Plate 77). Van Doesburg had been creating geometric abstracts as well. Upon seeing that their work was similar, the three artists decided to join forces. Along with the architects Oud, Wils, Van't Hoff, and Rietveld and the sculptor Georges Vantongerloo (1886–), they founded the group De Stijl and the magazine.

Mondrian followed Van der Leck's example and introduced the simple red, yellow, and blue rectangles into his own work. This made it possible for him to create an art with none of the despised reference to natural appearances. As a further refinement, in about 1920 Mondrian began to separate his rectangles with strong black vertical and horizontal bars (Plate 78). He explained that "the pictorial space became white, black or gray: the form became red, blue or yellow." Eventually his pictures were composed in the simplest way: the verticals contained primary colors, and the horizontals the "noncolors" (black, white, and gray). This balance of contrasts he named "neoplasticism."

Neoplasticism was to find its most logical outlet of expression in the architecture of De Stijl. The architectual style was basically a severe arrangement of cubes, with primary colors applied for contrast. The new architecture produced examples both in Holland and abroad and influenced such great contemporary architects as Le Corbusier, Gropius, and Mies van der Rohe.

78. ***Composition with Red, Yellow, and Blue,*** **by Piet Mondrian**

The "Peintres Maudits"

THE COLORFUL bohemian way of life in Paris is legendary. But after the turn of the century its carefree surface could not always disguise an increasingly sinister undercurrent of degradation and vice. Too frequently, drink and drugs went hand in hand with desperation and self-destruction. In France, an artist who loses control of his life, dissipates his talent, or ends in final misery is known as a *peintre maudit,* an "accursed" or "doomed painter." Four such men were Amedeo Modigliani (1884–1920), Chaim Soutine (1894–1943), Jules Pascin (1885–1930), and Maurice Utrillo (1883–1955).

In their homelessness, intensity, and the passionate involvement of their lives, they seemed to be haunted—even hunted. In 1906, Modigliani left his native Italy for Paris, where a combination of drinking, drug addiction, and reckless living was to kill him at the age of thirty-six. He was incredibly handsome, both shy and quarrelsome, yet capable of great charm and of dominating conversation. He was usually dressed respectably and cleanly, in contrast to most of the other aspiring young Parisian artists. (Picasso himself started a fashion by wearing a "monkey suit," a denim coverall, with a workman's cap while painting all night and a soft felt hat from Spain for "dressing up." Furthermore, after examining some American Civil War photographs at Gertrude Stein's, Picasso decided that he looked like Lincoln and changed his hair style in the hope that the resemblance might become even more noticeable.)

Modigliani was known to the artists who gathered around Picasso—it may have been at the suggestion of Picasso that he moved to Montmartre—but he was not one of them. In his early days in Paris he led a rather solitary life; nevertheless, he was as clear in his ambition to become an artist, in particular a sculptor, as any of them. His restless temperament had led him to Paris, where he could find the chaotic milieu in which it was necessary for him to live. Despite his increasing addiction to cheap wine and drugs, "Modi's" work got better and better. His chief interest continued to be sculpture. His drawings were mainly sketches for sculpture, and at night he would go out with a wheelbarrow to steal stone from building sites.

Modigliani found two art dealers and soon was no longer an unknown. He continued to draw feverishly, and out of his experiments his distinctive style began to emerge. Never without a sketch pad and pencil, he constantly made jottings of what he saw about him. And these were almost always of people: the human form was the main subject of his art. Portraits and nudes dominated his output. The fact that his painting depended heavily on drawing does not mean that Modigliani did not understand the qualities of paint; on the contrary, he made full use of painting techniques. The overall texture of his paintings is extremely varied, perfectly calculated and perfectly achieved. He always used a limited range of color and tones in his paintings. The quietly melancholy *Woman with a Tie* (Plate 79) is typical in this way. The subdued flesh tones and dominant greenish grays are brightened only by the sudden red touch of the mouth.

Modigliani's sculpture, too, shows him to be a master of textural effects. There has always been some difficulty in determining how many sculptures he created from 1912 on, and to what years they belong. It is certain that this date marked a brilliant change in his view of art and launched not only a new development in his own career but also in the whole course of European sculpture. His new constructions clearly testified that Modigliani had looked long and carefully at the art of the African primitive masters who were the current enthusiasm of the Paris avant-garde. But his works were in no sense copies, for each of them bears the genuine feeling of Modigliani's vivid personality. The lines of his sculpture have the same clean, precise qualities that are typical of his painting and draftsmanship (Plate 80).

It was not until this sculptural phase that Modigliani reached full maturity as a painter. Unlike so many of his contemporaries, he remained a basically representational painter, exploring the problems of portraiture and nude studies with great success. But Modigliani's way of life was so wildly undisciplined, and had been for so long, that he was unable to fight off the tuberculosis which killed him in 1920. He died in dreadful poverty.

modigliani

79. *Woman with a Tie,* by Amedeo Modigliani

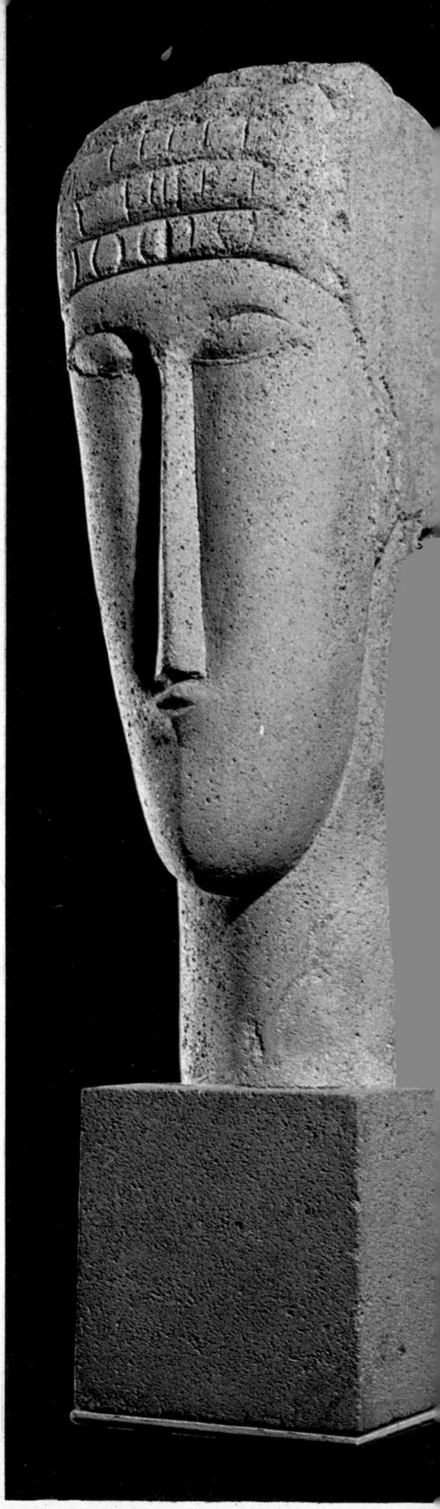

80. *Head,* by Amedeo Modigliani

Chaim Soutine, like Modigliani, showed all the signs of restless torment in his painting as in his life. Whereas Modigliani's canvases give the impression that he was able to achieve a temporary spiritual repose in his art, however, the paintings of Soutine reflect the tortured violence of his life. He painted with an almost insane ferocity. He once finished a picture and found afterward that, in painting it, he had seriously dislocated his thumb. The energy and concentration he brought to the creative act was so great that he was not aware of the mishap at the time.

Soutine came from a miserably poor Lithuanian Jewish family. The Jewish religious code of his boyhood was so strict that he was forbidden to draw or create any image whatsoever; but Soutine's passion to become an artist could not be suppressed. He stole crayons when he was seven and drew whenever he could. Having been expelled from school, he set out to study painting—first at Minsk, then at the School of Fine Arts in Vilna, and at last in Paris, where he arrived in 1913. But the École des Beaux-Arts was suited neither to Soutine's temperament nor to his strong ideas about painting. Soon he found a more sympathetic atmosphere in La Ruche ("The Beehive"), a studio block where Modigliani, Léger, and the Russian Jewish painter Marc Chagall (1887–) all lived. Modigliani, who was kind, sensitive, and always alert to other talents, introduced Soutine to his dealer Zborowski. Through this contact, Soutine was able to sell his first few paintings.

The paintings that Soutine did at La Ruche, though not yet formed in his mature manner, already have the terrifying emotional intensity that marks his style. These included a series of gladioli paintings of enormous power and some remarkable views of Montmartre. In his depiction of reality, Soutine distorted his forms with wild and rhythmic effect. This was carried almost to extremes in his important period at Céret, where, in his most productive phase (1920–1922), he finished over two hundred paintings. In their violent upheavals these remind one of nothing so much as earthquakes.

Soutine always painted directly from nature. This could cause practical difficulties, such as happened during the period when he was depicting slabs of butchered meat. At La Ruche, he had made friends with the employees of a local slaughterhouse and practiced painting pieces of beef that he got from them. In 1922 he painted an admirable *Side of Beef.* In 1925 he got his hands on the entire carcass of a steer and managed to get it up into his studio, where he worked at painting it for days on end. When the carcass got too dry in the heat, buckets of blood were brought from the slaughterhouse to pour over it. The paintings are full of rich, bloody colors. But not surprisingly, his neighbors complained loudly of the smell.

After the beef episode, Soutine did a number of pictures of plucked or halfplucked fowl (Plate 81). These are still life, but, more importantly, still life of flesh. Also at this time, Soutine was doing a series of portraits of youths in the uniforms of their work—pastry cooks, bellboys, and the like (Plate 82). Alone among Soutine's paintings in their charm and sentiment, these seem to have pleased everyone.

Soutine went on painting through the 1930's. His last great series was of tree-filled landscapes in which he seemed to return in spirit to the woodlands of his native Lithuania. Despite the danger to Jews, Soutine remained in France during World War II, and it was there that he died, before the war's end. It was an entirely appropriate gesture of Picasso to defy the regulations of the German occupation by joining in Soutine's funeral procession.

Jules Pascin, whose real name was Julius Pincas, was another artistic wanderer. A Bulgarian by birth, the son of a Sephardic Jew, he may have studied art in Vienna. It is impossible to say with certainty what his background was, since Pascin liked to cover his tracks and create an air of mystery about where he had come from and what he was doing. As a young man he lived in Munich, where he was well known for the clear, cynical drawings that he contributed to the magazine *Simplicissimus.* By 1905 he had arrived in Paris, and his early work there sometimes resembles that of the Fauves. A few years later a marked cubist tendency appeared in his style. But the artist with whom he had the most in common was Henri de Toulouse-Lautrec. Like Lautrec, Pascin had an interest in painting subjects from the world of low enter-

81. ***Dead Fowl,*** **by Chaim Soutine**

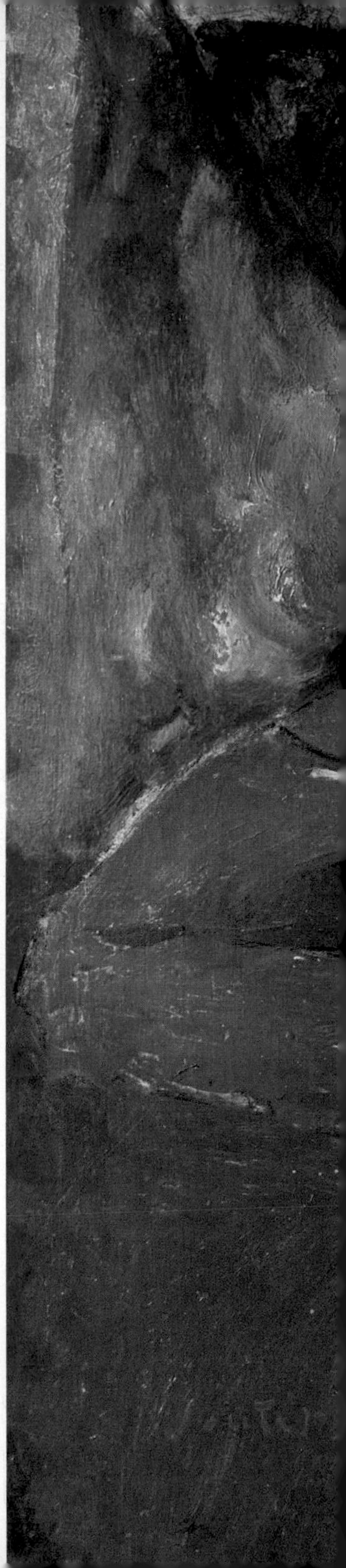

82. ***The Pageboy at Maxim's,*** **by Chaim Soutine**

tainment; like him, also, Pascin worked out a style of rapid sketching in a very fluid oil technique.

During these years he was probably better known in Germany than in France. In 1905 he exhibited at the famous Paul Kassiner Gallery in Berlin, alongside the work of Van Gogh and several others. In 1911 his pictures were shown at the Berlin Sezession exhibition and were considered to be in the line of German expressionism. In short, just as he had no personal roots, Pascin had no deep permanent artistic roots. When World War I broke out, to avoid being drafted by any European country, Pascin fled to the United States. In New York he had his first one-man show, but his sales were very poor. He decided to go south, traveling at various times to Mexico, Cuba, and New Orleans. On these trips he preferred to use watercolor or chalk-and-pencil overlaid with watercolor washes. These were ideal media for quick impressionistic note-taking.

It was typical of Pascin that he should have returned to Paris almost immediately after he became a naturalized American citizen. He was back in the French capital by 1920, the year Modigliani died. He never met the Italian artist, but he certainly took over from him as leading bohemian of the day. Pascin's work sold well during the 1920's, and he became famous for his lavish parties. During this period, female nudes and semi-nudes were his most usual subjects. More drawn than painted, they emerge in a delicate luminous glow from the shimmering light of the background (Plate 83). They appear casual, but actually many hours of work went into their seemingly spontaneous poses. While still in his early middle age, Pascin committed suicide in 1930.

A painter almost totally lacking in artistic purpose was Maurice Utrillo. It is hardly an exaggeration to say that he often painted pictures only to buy his next drink. When Modigliani first met Utrillo, he was obliged to pick him up off the floor of a bar and march off, carrying with him two bottles of wine. They ended that night, as well as many future ones, in the police station.

 Utrillo was born the illegitimate son of Suzanne Valadon

83. ***Mirelle,* by Jules Pascin**

(1867–1938), an acrobat turned artist's model. His mother, who frequently posed for Renoir, had artistic talent herself and was encouraged by her painter friends to develop it. Degas, the greatest draftsman of the age, gave her lessons. It was as a result of her interest in art that Utrillo was first given painting materials. The circumstances were not happy, for the paints were to provide occupational therapy for Utrillo, who was committed to a home for alcoholics at the age of eighteen. After taking some art lessons, he developed a facility for turning out a staggering number of scenes of his native Montmartre, the picturesque artistic colony where he was born and lived. In Utrillo's pictures the interest in humanity and self-expression that characterized the postimpressionist painters is not to be found. His compositions tend to follow a general set pattern. Usually, a broad expanse of road in the foreground recedes into the distance, and buildings close in the composition at both sides (Plate 84).

Utrillo's enormous output of paintings was a direct result of economic necessity, the extravagance of his way of life, and his constant need for drink. Even when he was briefly out of Paris, he painted the squares and streets he knew so well, from memory. He worked quickly to lay down a charcoal sketch on the canvas; next, he would rapidly paint in oils over the sketch, with a spontaneous technique that quite often became simply careless. At his best, however, Utrillo is an artist with pleasing qualities. His feeling for stonework and plastered buildings makes him a master of picturesque city scenes in many works.

84. ***Rue Norvins*****, by Maurice Utrillo**

Matisse, Dufy, and Derain

AFTER HIS heroic period as leader of the Fauves, Matisse arrived at a much more established position in the art world. By 1908, the cubists had taken over as leaders of the avant-garde. During the winter of 1907–1908 the famous Académie Matisse was organized. These new art classes attracted scores of students from America, Central Europe, and Scandinavia. Matisse taught in the same way that he had been instructed by Gustave Moreau. Like Moreau, Matisse had no wish to force old academic traditions on his students, nor did he encourage them to imitate his own style.

It was at this time that Matisse produced several important works. His qualities as draftsman, designer, and colorist can be seen in six paintings of this period which represent goldfish. In *Interior with Goldfish* (Plate 85), the three principal elements—the bowl of goldfish, the flowers, and the nude figure (which is a painting of one of his own sculptures, the *Reclining Nude* of 1907)—are perfectly balanced against one another. The design they form is not merely flat and ornamental. These juggling contrasts between a flatly colored decorative surface and the lively play of different elements against each other in depth are a characteristic feature of Matisse's style.

The *Decorative Figure on an Ornamental Background* (Plate 86), painted in 1927, is an amazingly brilliant work. Here, more than in any other of his paintings, the decorative and pattern-making aspect of Matisse's style is shown. For some years after this, Matisse turned away from easel paintings and concentrated on drawings, prints, and sculpture; but his best sculptures were probably those he had executed between 1909 and 1913, when he produced the *Jeannette* series, (Plate 87). Five heads progress from a fairly faithful likeness of a girl to a much freer, broken style in which natural forms are expressively distorted.

Whereas Matisse's art has an intensely emotional effect on the spectator, that of Dufy is lighter in feeling and slighter in signifi-

85. *Interior with Goldfish,* by Henri Matisse

86. *Decorative Figure on an Ornamental Background,* by Henri Matisse

87. *Jeannette IV,* by Henri Matisse

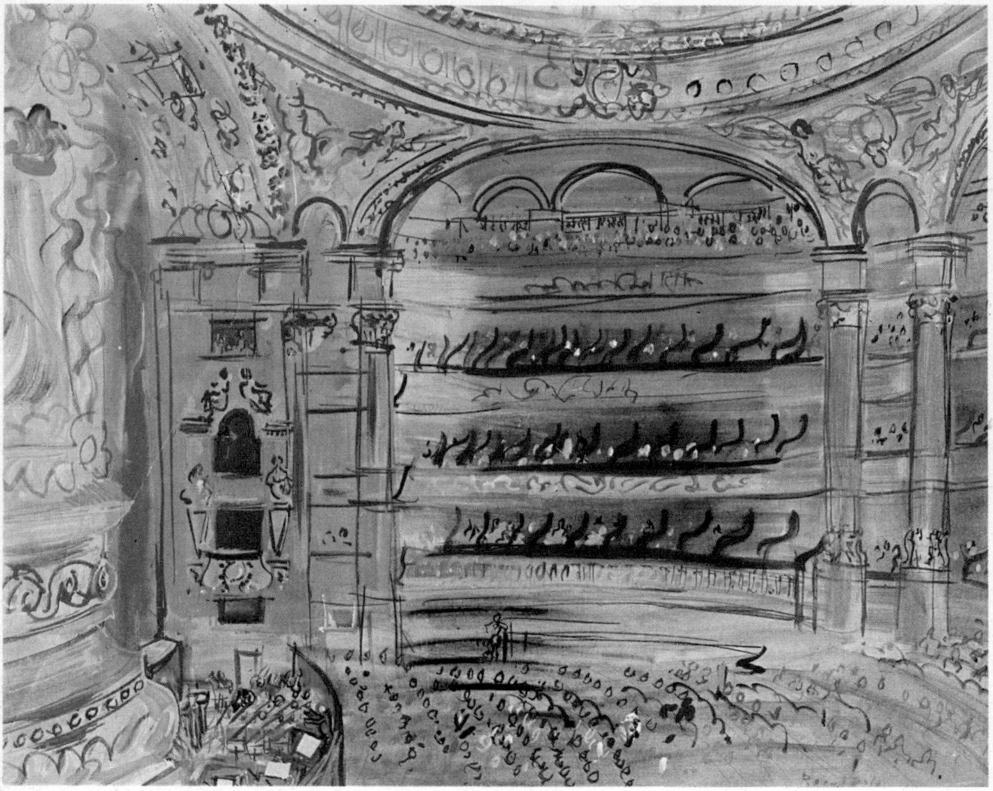

88. ***The Paris Opera House,*** **by Raoul Dufy**

cance. In about 1918, after much experimentation, Dufy returned to a more delicate Fauve style and began to paint pictures with an elegant scurrying of line over bright-colored wash backgrounds. After World War II, he spent some time in the United States, a country that fascinated him. There he worked on paintings of crowds, skyscrapers, prairie sunsets, and Arizona rodeos. But for the greater part of his life, Dufy remained faithful to a few themes in his paintings. Devoted to music, he painted pictures in homage to Mozart and Bach and delighted in painting orchestras, brass bands, and scenes at the opera (Plate 88). Other

89. ***Two Sisters,*** **by André Derain**

favorite subjects were the races and streets hung with bunting for celebrations. Dufy's work, if not so memorable as that of his more gifted and more serious contemporaries, always succeeds in captivating the spectator with its great charm.

André Derain's artistic career, like Dufy's, was launched as a Fauve. However, he was basically much more attracted to tradition than were most of his friends. He copied in the Louvre and never rejected the great paintings of the past. The example of the past perhaps led Derain to be a more cautious painter than any other of the Fauves. His later pictures lack Fauve vitality, and he has none of the intellectual quality of Matisse. His are respectful paintings, and it was no doubt a respect for the ordered discipline of cubism that led him to be influenced by that movement; but he did not remain a cubist for long. The example of the early French and Italian "primitives" and the art of the fifteenth century came to dominate his imagination after about 1920. Prior to that, the influence that classical painting had on his style can be seen in works such as *Two Sisters* (Plate 89). The pose of the two women is classical in attitude, but a new human sympathy is apparent in the treatment of these stark figures. It is to Derain's credit that, with so many different influences on his work, he managed to absorb them and yet keep a measure of his own individuality.

Picasso, Braque, and Leger

IN THE YEARS before 1925 Picasso was applying the innovations of cubism and developing the style with ever-increasing strength. In 1917 he traveled to Rome, Naples, and Florence with the French "jack-of-all-arts" Jean Cocteau (1889–1963). This trip had two effects on Picasso. First, he became interested in *commedia dell'-arte,* a traditional form of Italian theater in which the character Harlequin played a major role (Plate 90). Second, a deep appreciation for classical forms was revived in him. He began to paint many monumental female figures, either nude or in classical draperies. After the birth of his son in 1921, these impressive figures were often combined with others to portray the theme of motherhood.

Picasso next entered the phase of his career when he was associated in part with the surrealist movement. This movement, which we shall deal with presently, created a pictorial world of weird dreams and subconscious imagery.

The Muse (sometimes known as *Two Women;* Plate 91) is clearly a postcubist composition. In it, Picasso strives to reinterpret three-dimensionality; but its violent distortion is far more emotional, far less careful, than that of classical analytic cubism. The high point of this tendency is seen in *Guernica* (Plate 92), Picasso's passionate outcry against war. This greatest of all political paintings was produced during the Spanish Civil War. Picasso was horrified at the ruthless attack by fascist bombers that completely destroyed the ancient Basque capital, Guernica. He found this action not only horribly inhuman but also profoundly contradictory to the whole of Spanish history and culture. Thus, it is the ancient animal symbols of Spain that spell out the terrible catastrophe, that raise the painting from protest against a single event to an artistic statement of timeless significance. The gaping, disemboweled horse, the howling fleeing figures, the body of a

90. ***Harlequin at the Looking Glass,*** **by Pablo Picasso**

dead soldier, and the anguished women become images of all human suffering.

Of social conscience, Picasso hotly declared in 1945:

"What do you think an artist is? An imbecile who has only his eyes if he's a painter, or ears if he's a musician, or a lyre at every level of his heart if he's a poet, or even if he's a boxer, just his muscles? On the contrary, he's at the same time a polit-

91. *The Muse,* by Pablo Picasso
92. *Guernica* (detail), by Pablo Picasso

ical being, constantly alive to heartrending, fiery or happy events, to which he responds in every way. How would it be possible to feel no interest in other people and by virtue of an ivory indifference to detach yourself from the life which they so copiously bring you? No, painting is not done to decorate apartments. It is an instrument of war for attack and defense against the enemy."[1]

This mood in Picasso's paintings continued throughout World War II. He was in Paris during the whole of the German occupation and refused to collaborate with the Vichy government or the Nazis in any way.

Before 1914, Picasso and Braque had lived and worked like Siamese twins but, as Picasso rather mysteriously said later, "When the mobilization started I sent Braque and Derain to the station. I have never seen them since." Thus an era ended. Braque was sent to the front, was wounded, and was commended for his bravery. He began painting again in 1917, but this time alone, for Picasso had moved far beyond him. Braque's cubism now became much freer and easier than before, particularly in his landscapes. His still lifes from this postwar period (Plate 95) are graceful in effect, with none of the classical analytic cubist period. Their color is more varied, and the drawing is more expressive. In his last years Braque developed still further. *Wheat Field* (Plate 96), a late work of 1952, shows an expressive use of rich and heavy textures, with abstract tendencies very like post-World War II American painting.

Fernand Léger came in contact with cubism in 1910, the year

[1] In the light of Picasso's heroic statment, the works of two Mexican painters should be mentioned here—Diego Rivera (1886–1957) and David Alfaro Siqueiros (1898–   ). Mexico has long been known as a home of strong political passions. Rivera was able to combine politics and painting successfully in vast murals such as *The Mexican War of Independence* (Plate 93). Siqueiros, who led a students' strike at his art school at the age of fifteen, later joined the Mexican revolutionary army. He dedicated all his life to both painting and revolutionary politics, and for this he spent much time in prison. The furious character of his painting reflects the way he lived; certainly, *Echo of a Scream* (Plate 94) could not be more passionate in its message.

93. ***The Mexican War of Independence,*** **by Diego Rivera**

that he met Picasso and Braque. He did not adopt their style, but borrowed from it. His simplifications have a special quality about them, a tooled metallic feeling; the different parts seem as if bolted together by an engineer (Plate 97). And indeed it was things like locomotive wheels, parts of complex machines, and bicycles that fascinated Léger. He had been drafted in 1914, and during the war he made many drawings of soldiers and weapons. These had a great effect on both his style and subject matter.

After 1921, human figures that did look as if made of iron began to play a larger role in his painting. These images, which never completely displaced machines in his work, are monumental and have an unnatural stability.

94. *Echo of a Scream,* by David Alfaro Siqueiros

95. *Still Life on a Marble Table,* by Georges Braque

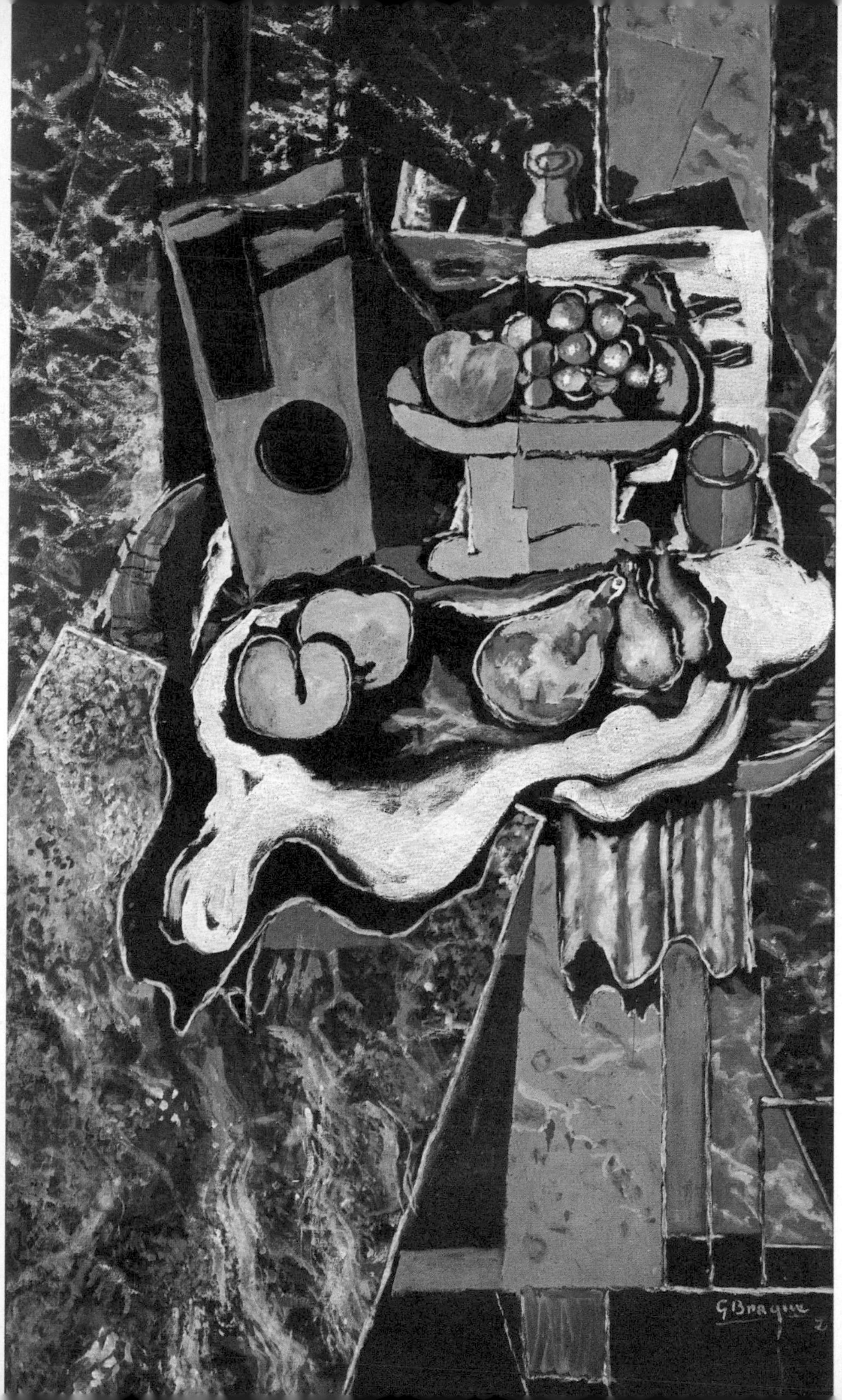
G Braque

97. *Soldiers Playing Cards,* by Fernand Léger

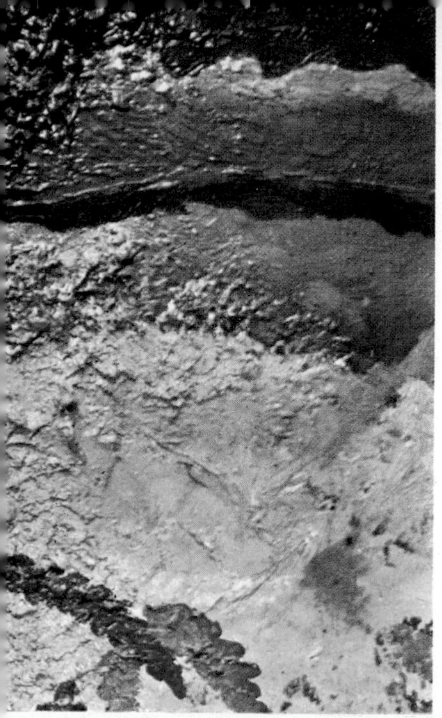

96. *Wheat Field,* by Georges Braque

98. ***Leisure: Homage to Louis David,*** **by Fernand Léger**

It was on his return to Paris from the United States after World War II that Léger completed the series *Leisure* (Plate 98). Popular pastimes had always attracted him as subject matter, and he did many paintings of cyclists (cycle racing then being the French national sport), as well as of soccer teams. In depicting such themes, as elsewhere, Léger participated in the life of his times and in modern discoveries with a kind of determined simplicity.

Chagall and Klee

EUROPEAN PAINTING, from the Renaissance through cubism, had been based on depiction of the visible world within the bounds of logic and normal perception. This long tradition meant absolutely nothing to Marc Chagall, and in his lopsided universe houses are built upside down, fish play the fiddle, and cows can fly.

Chagall was born in Vitebsk, a small Russian town in which half the population was Jewish. His childhood was filled with Jewish voices and Jewish faces, and in the tight community of small streets he could watch the dramas of the people around him. There were wedding processions, with musicians and dancing. There were market days when the Russian peasants would come in with their produce, bringing with them fields, skies, stars, and the warm vigor of people of the land. Chagall's family was poor. They ate herring, pickles, black bread and butter; and on the Sabbath his father, to young Marc's envy, would eat meat. Often there was only millet and barley meal to eat.

The feast days, with their colors and their banquets, deeply impressed Chagall, as did the candles for the dead climbing in a blaze toward the synagogue on the Day of Atonement. Most important of all to him was his family. It was large—aunts, uncles, and grandparents all being part of the family folklore that Chagall cherished in his imagination. On the throne of his family sat his energetic mother. His father was a quiet man whose smile, Chagall said, "whispered of the street where the dim passers-by roamed about, reflecting the moonlight."

There were others, such as Uncle Neuch, with whom Chagall used to ride and who played the violin like a gypsy. There was his grandfather, who spent half his life on top of the stove and who once was discovered sitting on the rooftop munching carrots. All these images were to provide Chagall with a lifetime's inspiration.

But in a Russian Jewish community it was impossible to become a painter; therefore Chagall, like Soutine, left for Paris. There he met the writer Max Jacob, Delaunay, Modigliani, and Apollinaire. The year in which Chagall arrived in Paris, 1910, was the same year in which Picasso completed his cubist masterpiece *Woman with a Mandolin.* The city's artistic life was then dominated by the experiments of the cubist painters. Chagall learned a firmer sense of form from these painters.

Chagall suffered greatly from homesickness in Paris. All the time he was there he continued to paint poetic, dreamlike memories of his native village. Of the paintings of this period, only *Paris through the Window* (Plate 99) takes the city as its subject and, moreover, betrays his uneasiness there. An atmosphere of muffled panic is felt. The double-faced man with the blue profile is masked, the sphynxlike cat registers alarm, and a train runs upside down. In the background are two small prone figures, seemingly knocked down or dead; above them, a parachutist descends perilously. Shafts of color, like searchlight beams, split the sky. The whole effect of this brightly hued picture is disturbing.

Chagall left early in 1914 and went to Berlin for his first one-man exhibit. The outbreak of war sent him home to Vitebsk, where he married his adored Bella, the girl to whom he had been engaged before going to Paris.

Suddenly, after the 1917 revolution, Chagall became a respected artistic figure in Russia. Offered a post as Minister of Arts, he preferred instead to return to Vitebsk in a lesser official capacity and founded a school of fine arts. Because he had no gift for administration or party politics, this episode ended in semicomic disaster—his pupils and professors finally rebelled and sent him packing to Moscow. There he was asked to do murals for the State Jewish Theater. These he executed in a revolutionary manner that gave free rein to his fantasy and imagination. With these works, he had arrived at his mature style.

Back in Paris in 1922, Chagall's color grew progressively richer. With increasing assurance, he started to play on the recurring themes that his intensely poetic imagination suggested to him. Acrobats, trapeze artists, and other circus performers became favorite subjects. There are also many paintings representing Bella and himself reclining or embracing amid enormous bouquets

99. ***Paris through the Window*****, by Marc Chagall**

of flowers. *To My Wife* (Plate 100), a richly crowded composition, belongs to this series. Painted shortly after his wife died, it is both a tribute to her and a summary of his life's work.

Another painter remarkable for the charm and fantasy of his

100. ***To My Wife,*** **by Marc Chagall**

work was Paul Klee. He resembled Chagall in his mastery of an imaginative world which is childlike, rather than childish. While taking this seemingly unsophisticated approach to painting, Klee also was fully capable of dealing with adult emotions.

Klee took a long time to reach his mature style. He started in Munich and, under the influence of the decadent symbolism of Franz von Stuck (1863–1928), produced thin and wiry drawings

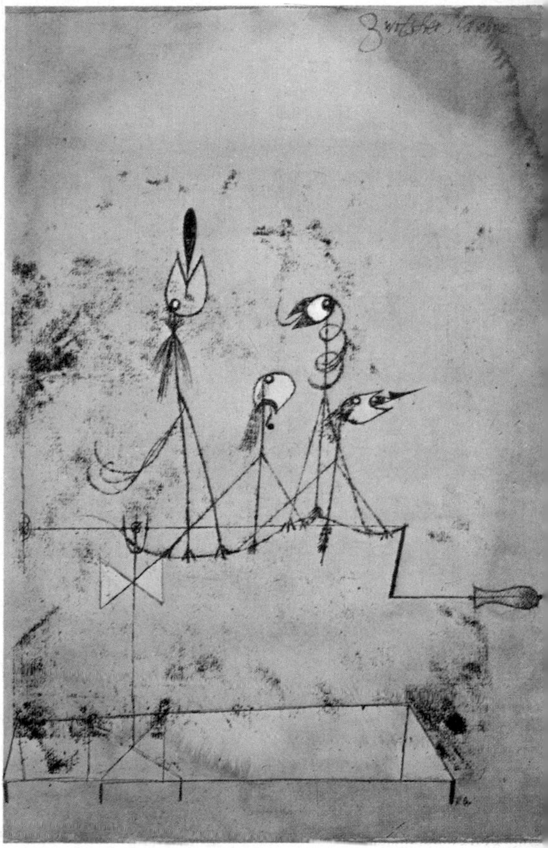

101. ***The Twittering Machine,*** **by Paul Klee**

reflecting turn-of-the-century German Jugendstil. From 1912, Klee was associated with the Blaue Reiter and became a close friend of its founders, Kandinsky and Marc. Through this association, he began to depend more on abstract form to express inner emotions. More important than his contact with the Blaue Reiter, perhaps, was his trip to Tunisia in 1914. He stayed only twelve days, but the rich visual experience of North Africa changed his attitudes radically. Previously he had concentrated on line and occasional watercolor washes. Now he was able to write in his diary, "Color and I are one: I am a painter."

Late in 1920 Klee was invited to teach at the Bauhaus in Weimar. This school of design had been founded the year before by the architect Walter Gropius. The Bauhaus curriculum wished to establish a closer relationship between architecture, the arts, and industrial design. In their own words, its members were attempting to "reestablish the harmony between the different artistic activities, between craftsmanship and artistry, and [to] bind them all together in a new conception of building." Klee taught there for ten years. With its reactionary official artistic policies, Nazi rule in Germany meant that the Bauhaus eventually had to close down (1933). Klee, who in 1931 had become a professor at the Düsseldorf Academy, was suspect for his modernism and was forced to return to his native Switzerland in 1933. He lived there until his death in 1940.

An early entry in Klee's diary gives a clue to the development of his career. In 1902 he wrote: "I want to be as though newborn, knowing nothing about Europe, nothing, knowing no pictures, entirely impulses, almost in an original state!" As an artist, Klee was both very personal in his expression and socially oriented in aims. Very often his paintings are completely nonrepresentational or are composed of baffling forms whose meaning seems to escape us. An air of mystery is often strangely combined with his frankly childlike images. Furthermore, what may seem to be something breezily spontaneous in the finished work was actually calculated with extreme care by the artist.

Klee described his drawing as "taking a line for a walk." Often his drawings are full of wit and humor. *The Twittering Machine* (Plate 101), for example, pokes fun at both mechanized society and the futurist movement. *Highways and Byways* (Plate 102), however, is an impression of an actual Egyptian landscape the artist visited on a trip in 1928–1929. Klee never failed to transform his gentle and almost faint outlines into forms that are highly meaningful.

102. ***Highways and Byways,*** **by Paul Klee**

Morandi and Italian Metaphysical Painting

A FEELING for the mysterious significance of form is characteristic, in a different way, of the best paintings of the Italian painter Giorgio Morandi (1890–). This is particularly true of his haunting still lifes of bottles. His fellow-painter Giorgio de Chirico (1888–) wrote of Morandi, "He sees with the eyes of a man who believes; the inner framework of things that are dead for us, because motionless, appears to him under its most comforting aspect, under its eternal aspect." Morandi's more classic still lifes are almost always successful, particularly in his masterful handling of grainy textures (Plate 103). He has also painted a number of quiet and delicate landscapes; these and the still lifes have put him in the front rank of modern Italian painters. In some of his earlier works there is evidence of the influence of the metaphysical painters (Plate 104).

Metaphysical painting was very largely an Italian development. (A formal definition of "metaphysics" is "the branch of philosophy which studies the ultimate nature of existence.") The driving force behind it was Giorgio de Chirico. The painting of this school is at its best when closest to the blank, airless, somehow menacing atmosphere of *Nostalgia of the Poet* (Plate 105). The emphasis in metaphysical painting on empty streets, abandoned railway stations, and a general feeling of being lost or out of place can be traced back to De Chirico and the circumstances of his youth.

Giorgio de Chirico spent the first years of his life in Greece, where his father was supervising the construction of a railroad line. There he received some elementary lessons in art, but he produced little to suggest that he was exceptionally talented. Returning to Italy after his father's death, he moved from city to

103. ***Still Life,*** **by Giorgio Morandi**

city. He was always in his mother's company and never stayed in any one place for long.

It was in Paris that he began to make out what he described as

104. ***Still Life with Manikin,*** **by Giorgio Morandi**

"the first ghosts of a more complete, more profound and more complicated art, an art which was—in one word—more *metaphysical.*" His paintings were now concerned with empty streets, gloomy statuary, puzzling figures and situations. The emphasis was always on desertion. Human beings scarcely exist in De Chirico's art. He shows us only the shell of life—man-made ob-

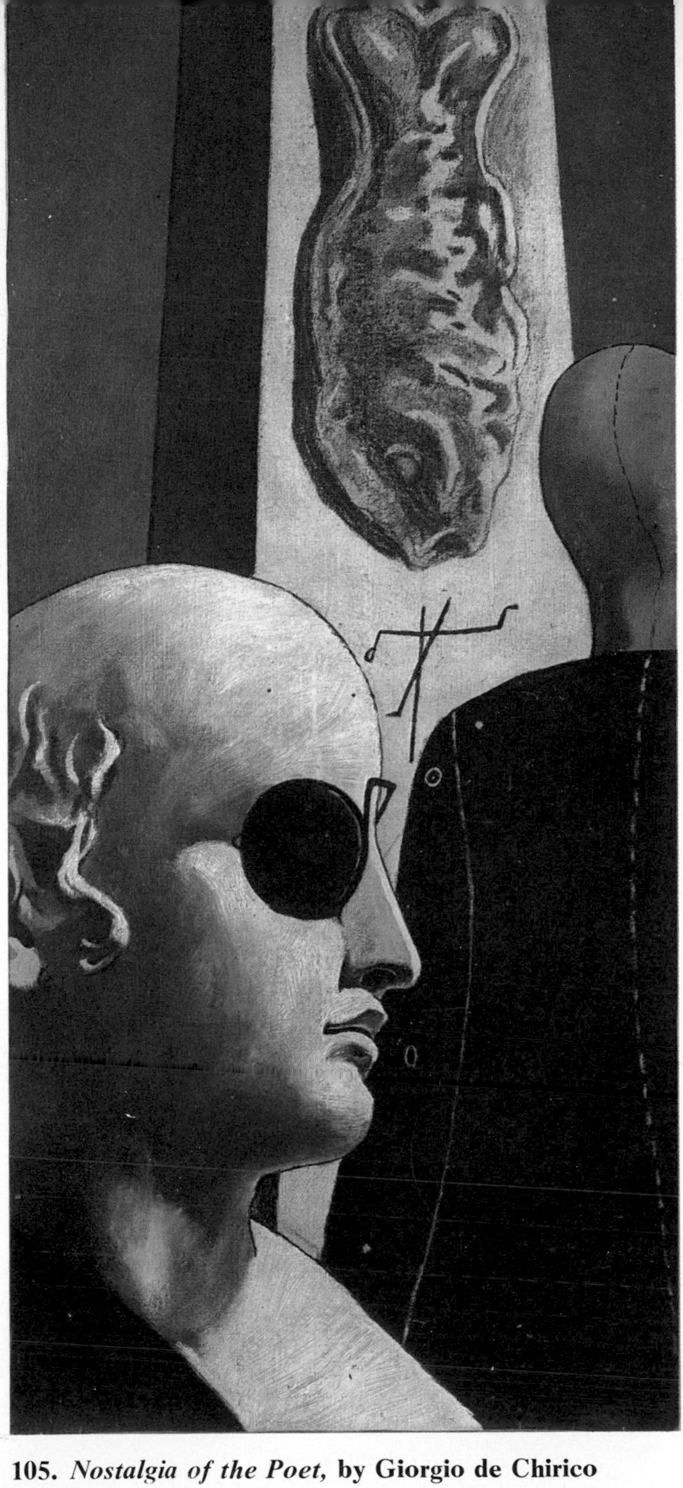

105. *Nostalgia of the Poet,* by Giorgio de Chirico

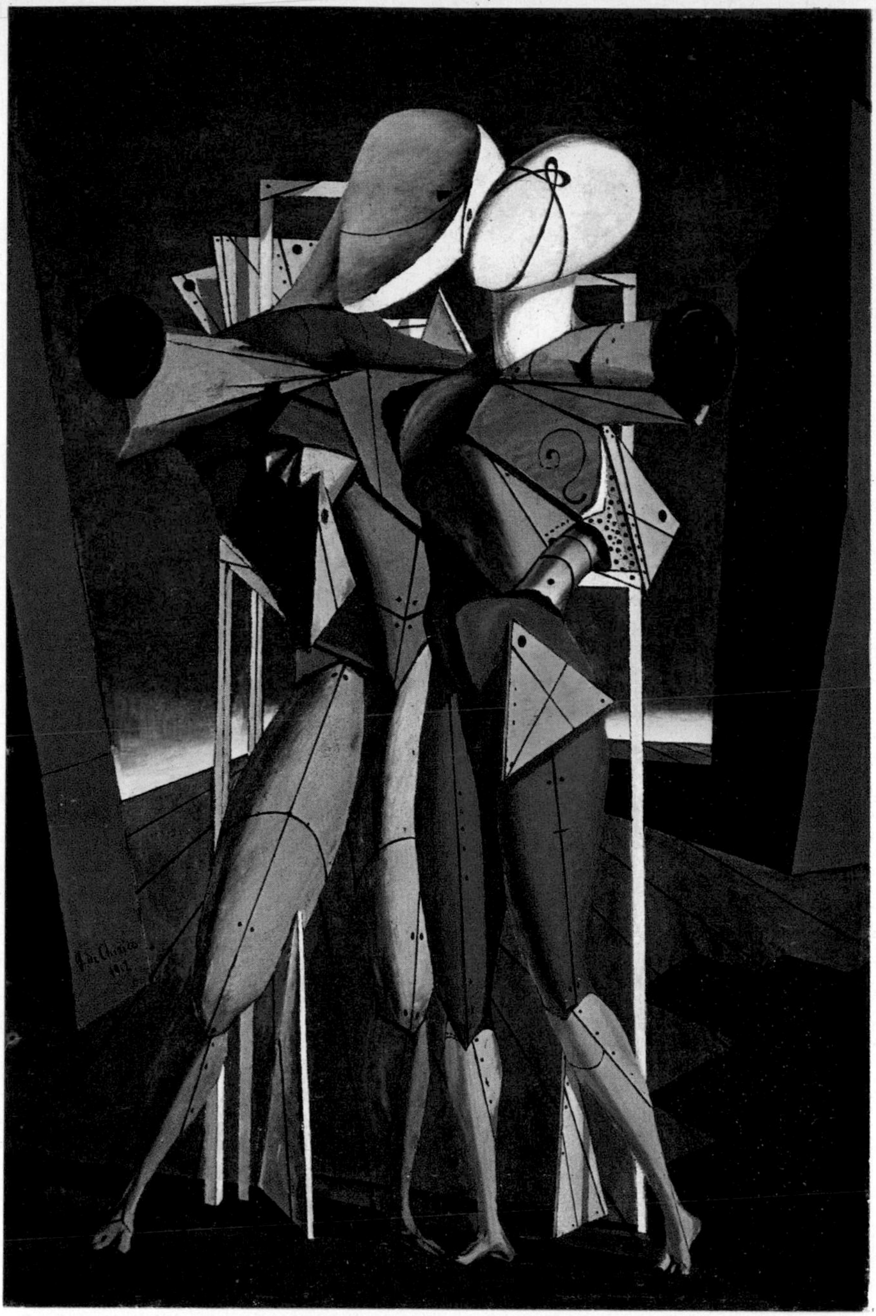

106. *Hector and Andromache,* by Giorgio de Chirico

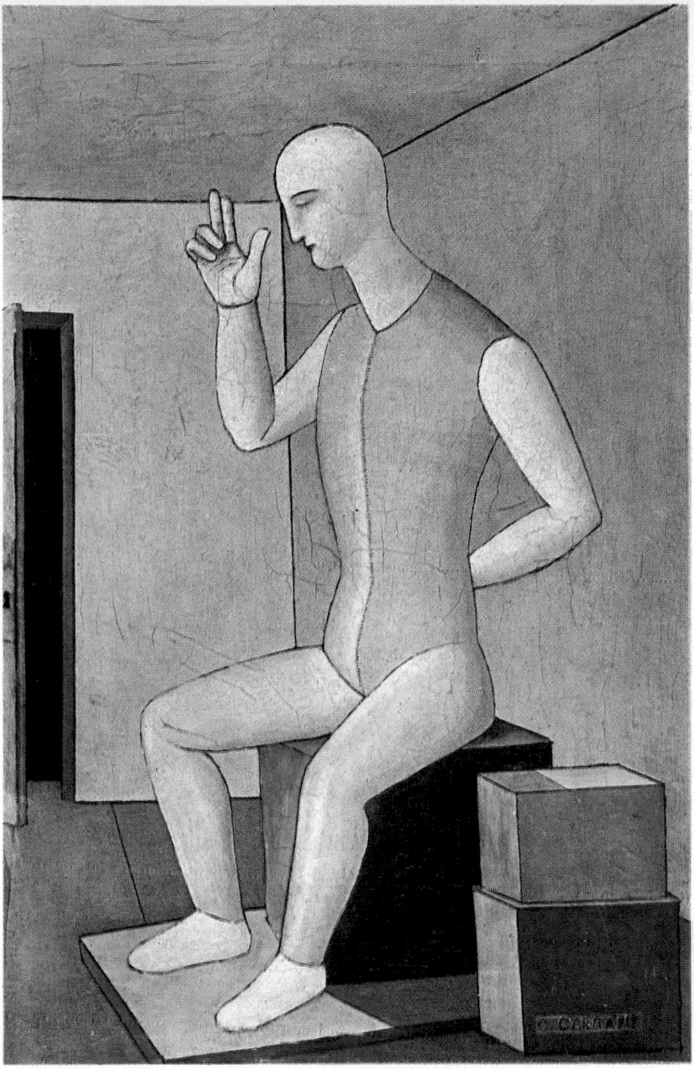

107. ***The Hermaphrodite Idol,*** **by Carlo Carrà**

jects and inanimate beings from whom human feeling has been mystifyingly stripped away.

These unusual landscapes were followed, about the time of the outbreak of World War I, by a concentration on a hodgepodge of objects such as gloves, cigar boxes, and hands from anatomical models. It was at this time, also, that manikins first appeared in his work. These manikins bear a strong resemblance to the jointed ones used by artists for sketching proportions or physical movement. In the paintings they become creatures with no human concerns, yet are an eerie kind of second-hand approximation of human forms (Plate 106).

The war again forced the De Chirico family to return to Italy, and Giorgio was drafted into the Italian army. Confined to a military hospital, he met Carlo Carrà (already discussed in connection with the futurist movement). Carrà's enthusiasm for that determinedly dynamic style had died down, and he was ready for a change. Painting side by side with De Chirico in the hospital, he adopted the metaphysical style (Plate 107). An entertaining note is that the staff doctors thought they might be off their heads.

Carrà took over many motifs (specific themes or subjects) from De Chirico, as did Morandi, briefly the third member of their group. But neither of them was able to develop the metaphysical style any further. Nor, it would seem, could De Chirico himself; his later work grew flabby and lacked the power of his earlier fantasies. When he started to reinterpret the masters of the Renaissance, his once devoted followers, the surrealists (champions of fantastic art), turned on him. In their 1928 exhibition, having called him a coward, a cheat, and a viper, the younger painters assembled a model entitled *Here Lies Giorgio de Chirico.* This was a cheap plaster reproduction of the leaning tower of Pisa surrounded by little rubber horses and doll furniture. These spiteful references to certain themes in De Chirico's work show the mixture of malice and childishness typical of many of the quarrels within surrealist groups.

Dada

WHAT THE word *Dada* means, or who made it up, remains obscure to this day. This would have appealed to the originators of the movement, who, in 1916, gathered together in Zurich at the Café Voltaire. Like surrealism, the movement was as much concerned with literature as with painting. Its originators, exiles and refugees, were equally rootless.

The Café Voltaire group was founded by Hugo Ball (1886–1927), a German writer who later became a religious recluse. He was joined by the jovial Romanian poet Tristan Tzara (1896–1968) and the painters Jean Arp (1887–1966) and Marcel Janco (1895–). Their method was to shock, and their aim was to lead an artistic revolt that would question the basis and deny the very existence of art.

Meetings at the Café Voltaire featured music and songs, and also such novelties as poems composed only of vowels. Absurd and only partly planned performances—the ancestors of recent "happenings"—broke out regularly. From this volatile background came the magazine *Dada,* which was almost entirely the creation of Tzara. The typography was scattered haphazardly across the page, and while the magazine had a certain flair, its editorial policy was to be against everything, no matter what. Thus the Dada manifesto tiresomely proclaimed: "Dada means nothing!" Other irksome discoveries included such axioms as "Thought is produced in the mouth." Typical Dada poems, shrieked or bellowed at the top of the lungs to startled audiences, had such memorable lines as "gadji beri bimba glandridi lanla louni caltori."

This forthright rejection of all the accepted standards of the European cultural tradition spread from Zurich to Berlin, Cologne, and Paris and finally to New York. Dada had a surprisingly profound effect on the painting—or rather, "anti-painting"—of the time.

In Cologne, Kurt Schwitters (1887–1948) founded his own branch of Dada, which he called "Merz" ("rubbish"). He constructed his art from bits and pieces found in the streets. Streetcar tickets, broken shoelaces, dirty feathers, wrapping paper—anything that had been thrown away as useless he collected avidly and transformed into collages (Plate 108). Their creation was his most important artistic activity, but he also wrote poetry and plays and tirelessly publicized Dada.

As a thoroughgoing rejecter of the world's standards, Francis Picabia (1879–1953) should have received some kind of special award. He was rich, rootless, eccentric, and quite frankly unable

108. ***Composition,*** **by Kurt Schwitters**

to see any meaning in the world or in art. Art, he said, must be "useless and impossible."

Picabia had nothing but sneering contempt for painting and for those who respected it. A talented painter as a child, he replaced his grandfather's old masters with his own copies; he then sold the originals to raise funds to enlarge his stamp collection. Later, he began attaching meaningless titles such as *Edtaonise* to his paintings and proclaimed that the title had more value than the picture. This was not the case, however, with *L'Enfant Carburateur* ("The Baby Carburetor" Plate 109). Here the carefully balanced abstract structure and the precision of the diagram dis-

109. *L'Enfant Carburateur,* by Francis Picabia

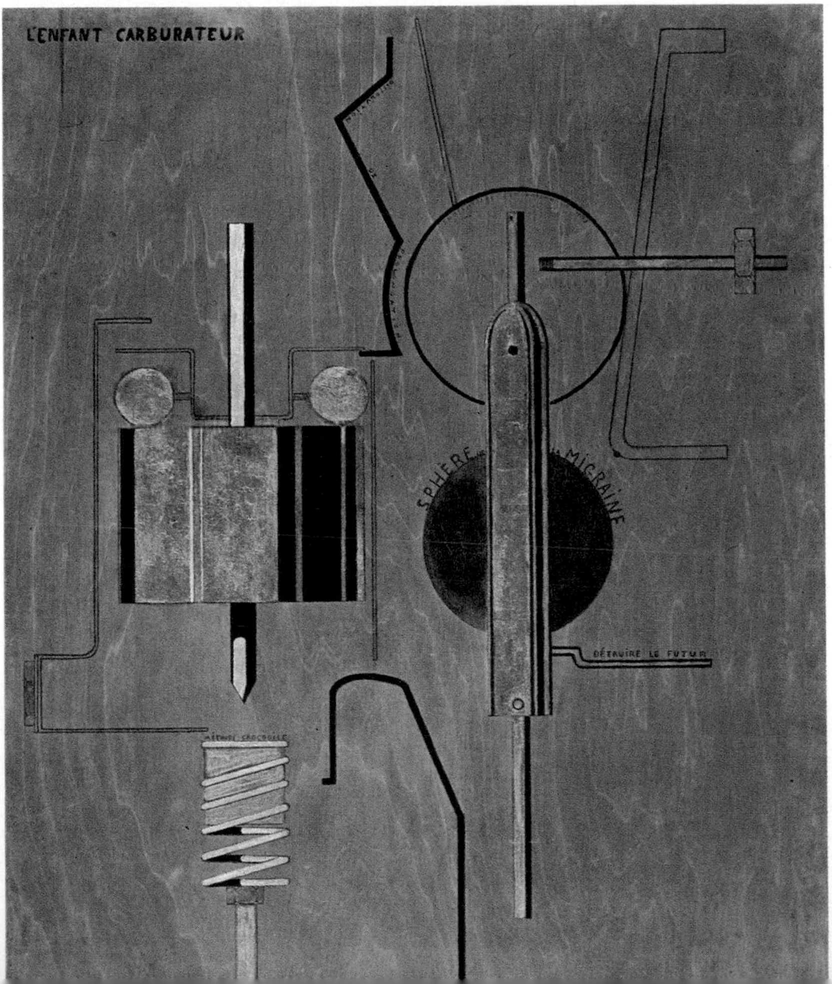

110. ***The Bride Stripped Bare by Her Bachelors, Even,*** **by Marcel Duchamp**

guise just one slight flaw: namely, that this machine has no meaning or no practical function whatsoever.

In Barcelona, he produced his own Dada periodical called *391* (once again, named for no particular reason). It contained not only his own restless semimechanical drawings but also poems by Apollinaire and Max Jacob and cubist drawings by Picasso and Braque. The police ran Picabia out of Spain. Without a backward glance he departed for America, where he was met by his old friend Marcel Duchamp, the greatest of all Dada artists.

Duchamp's association with Dada became suddenly apparent when he rejected his Section d'Or tradition by mounting a bicycle wheel on a wooden chair. This flash of inspiration was followed by his painting a moustache and an obscene pun on a reproduction of the *Mona Lisa.* Next, he exhibited such objects as a bottle rack, a hat stand, and a shovel. These last were all ordinary manufactured items, generally bought on sale, which Duchamp merely signed. Needless to say, their exhibition brought into question exactly what could be considered art. Duchamp simply called them his "ready-mades."

At the same time that he was collecting these articles and transforming them, merely by choosing them, into "ready-mades," Duchamp was embarking on his major work. This was the famous *Bride Stripped Bare by her Bachelors, Even* (Plate 110), an extremely complicated work that took twelve years to bring to what Duchamp called "a state of final incompletion." It consisted of two large sheets of glass, to which were added oil paint, lead wire, foil, dust, and varnish. Typically, he announced that the painting was "finished" only when it was accidentally cracked in 1926.

After this "anti-triumph" of anti-art, Duchamp gave up his artistic activities in favor of chess and very rarely produced new works. These later works also show him to be one of the most prophetic artists of this century, for in his whirling *Rotoreliefs* (1935) and *Fluttering Hearts* (1936) he anticipated both kinetic art and "pop" art by several decades.

Surrealism

André Breton (1896–1966), Louis Aragon (1897–), and Philippe Soupault (1897–)—none of them more than twenty-five years old at the time—were responsible for the first outbreak of surrealism in Paris. Together these three young poets ran the magazine *Littérature,* which was itself a fairly traditional journal. Dada had made an impact on their imaginations and led them to start their own rebellion. They broke with the Dadaists because they could not accept Dada's waywardness and anarchy.

The new group subscribed wholeheartedly to the values of dream worlds, folly, and madness. They were convinced that deliberate rejection of logical processes of thought and artistic creation would lead to a new kind of art. "We are still living under the reign of logic," complained Breton in the first surrealist manifesto in 1924. It was a reign that he felt to be tyrannical. "I believe," he continued, "in the future transmutation [i.e., synthesis] of those two seemingly contradictory states, dream and reality, into a sort of absolute reality of *surreality,* so to speak." The word "surrealism" had been coined previously by Apollinaire.

True freedom of the imagination was to be found both in the intense, feverish visions of such surrealist heroes as the poets Arthur Rimbaud and Gérard de Nerval, or in the world of dreams. Poetry and painting alike should be irrational and should shock or startle the senses. "Beauty," said Breton, "will be convulsive or it will not be."

Breton had studied medicine and worked with mentally disturbed soldiers during World War I. Freud's psychological theories and discoveries he knew well. Sometimes during analysis, the military patients had been encouraged to daydream and play free-association word games; and Breton thought these methods could be used in artistic creation. He described how he came to make his first experiments in this direction. As he was dropping off to sleep one night, he heard a curious phrase, "as if it had knocked on the window-pane." Something said to him distinctly, "There's a man cut in two by the window." This was followed up by a clear visual impression of the unfortunate incident. Soon after, Breton began writing whatever came into his head—on good days, fifty pages at a time.

Sharing Breton's unusual opinions was Max Ernst (1891–), a painter who, as he obscurely phrased it, tried to express in his work "the irritation of my visionary faculties." Ernst was the first true surrealist artist.

In 1922, using what amounted to a Dada technique, Ernst began creating collages with scraps of illustrations from old books. He believed these chance combinations could give a poetic reinterpretation of the real world. He welcomed hallucinations. In 1925, as he was staring at the wood-grain swirls of a hotel floor, strange images appeared to him. He placed sheets of paper on the floor and rubbed over them with graphite. (Rubbings like these are called "frottages"; by putting a piece of paper on a penny and rubbing over it with a pencil, anybody can make one.) Looking at these, Ernst said, "I was surprised by the sudden strengthening of my visionary faculties and by hallucinatory sequence of images." This deliberate release from the real world led to the terrifying landscapes of his most typical work. *The Eye of Silence* (Plate 111), for example, shows an unearthly region that seems to be covered with a veil of fungus or evil moss.

Joan Miró (1893–) is a lighter and happier painter in a more or less surrealist vein. Commuting between his native Barcelona and Paris in the years before 1925, he absorbed the examples of cubism, Kandinsky's abstractions, and Klee's highly personal childlike forms. These influences helped to form Miró's distinctive style—a style of great freedom and poetic, playful associations (Plates 112, 113). But it was his contacts with the surrealists that had a decisive influence on his art. Miró never numbered actively among the surrealists, although he was often associated with their movement. From them Miró learned the value of the subconscious, and in his works he often achieves what Breton had called the basic aim of surrealism: uniting the "surreal" (a com-

111. ***The Eye of Silence,* by Max Ernst**

bination of supernatural and subconscious imagery) with the real. Even Miró's most outlandish figures give the impression of inhabiting the real world. This was true also of his fellow-Spaniard Picasso during the brief phase when his work was influenced by the surrealists, as may be seen in his *Figures on a Beach.*

The best-known of the surrealists is yet another Spaniard,

112. *Large Composition*, by Joan Miró

113. *Man and Dog in Front of the Sun*, by Joan Miró

114. ***Premonition of Civil War,*** **by Salvador Dali**

Salvador Dali (1904–), an extroverted and self-publicizing artist. As a child he had been wild, talented, and impossibly spoiled. Indulged by his parents, he was permitted to do whatever he liked, whenever he liked. The young Dali was expelled as a show-off from every art school he attended; somehow, this did not disturb the course of his artistic development. At the San Fernando Institute in Madrid, he met the great Spanish poet Federico García Lorca and the film director Luis Buñuel, with whom Dali was later to create an artistic uproar. In 1923 he was thrown out of the institute for inciting a rebellion. In the same year he came across some reproductions of the works of De Chirico and Carrà in the Italian magazine *Valori Plastici.* The mysteriousness of their metaphysical painting gave him a new artistic impulse.

As decisive as this discovery were his trips to Paris in 1927 and 1928. Visited by Paul Eluard and his wife Gala at his home in

Cadaqués, Spain, Dali fell in love with Gala and eventually married her. Back in Paris, in 1928–1930, Dali collaborated with his friend Buñûel in making some of the first surrealist films, *Un Chien andalou* and *L'Age d'or* ("An Andalusian Dog" and "The Golden Age"). Both were brought out with as much surrealist fanfare as possible, and the scandalous nature of the films increased the public furor. *L'Age d'or,* the first feature-length surrealist film (in which Max Ernst starred as the leader of a band of outlaws), was sabotaged at its premiere by a right-wing political group. At a given signal, ink bottles were thrown at the screen, the audience was assaulted, and paintings by Dali, Miró, Ernst, and Yves Tanguy were trampled underfoot.

Surrealism thrived on such events. Its public image needed continual feeding by such personalities as Dali, who wore extraordinary clothes and a waxed moustache like a pitchfork and gave lectures at the university with one foot soaking in a bowl of ass's milk. He could always be relied on not to behave conventionally.

Dali's best and most characteristic surrealist period came when he returned to Spain with Gala. There they settled at Port Lligat, a tiny, poverty-stricken fishing village. Dali rented a shack from a crazed old fisherwoman named Lydia, who appears in many of his paintings of the time. In these paintings he set about transforming and intensifying the poverty, madness, and violence of the village. He turned the steep rocks and harsh sunsets into deeply receding landscapes of a black-magic world. In this frightening surrealist world, giraffes burn, half-eaten telephones lie on the beach, and pocket watches melt in the unnatural heat. Looming above, disturbing shapes disfigure the calm of the sky (Plate 114). All these strange elements were painted in a minutely realistic way.

Following sharp disagreements with Breton, Dali divorced himself from the surrealist movement. He continued to paint in much the same general manner, but with increasingly weaker effect. His landscape backgrounds, empty and haunted, were derived from the paintings of Yves Tanguy (1900–1955), who was an early member of the surrealist group. Entirely self-taught, Tanguy began painting in 1924 when he saw one of De Chirico's works. His

115. ***Fear,*** **by Yves Tanguy**

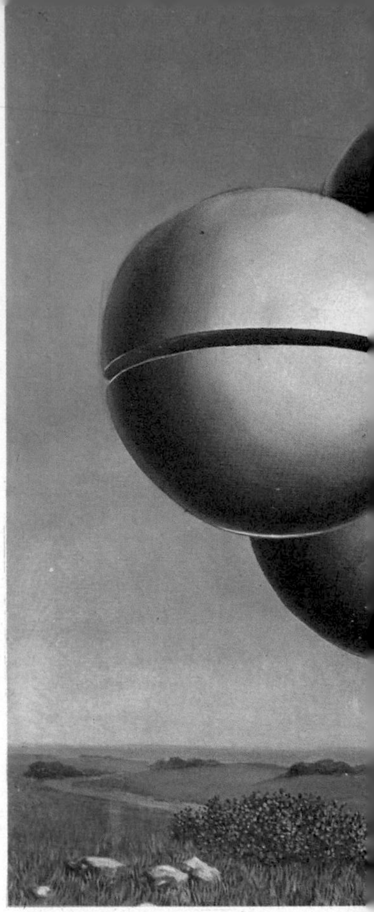

116. ***Voice of the Winds,*** **by René Magritte**

great theme was the infinity of space. In *Fear* (Plate 115) one cannot even guess at distance from or over the horizon, for the horizon itself does not exist. This is a convincing pictorial representation of a mystery.

If Tanguy seems to have constructed a totally different universe, the Belgian René Magritte (1898–1967), instead subtly introduces peculiar elements into the affairs of everyday life. He is more concerned with showing how near the surreal is to ordinary life than with Breton's attitude of meshing the real and the surreal. His quietly menacing pictures seem full of warnings or premonitions. The *Voice of the Winds* (Plate 116) is so calm and assured in its somewhat "science fiction" matter-of-factness that we are

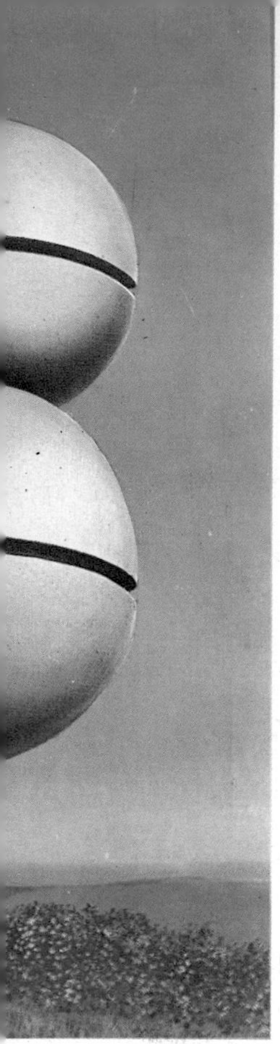

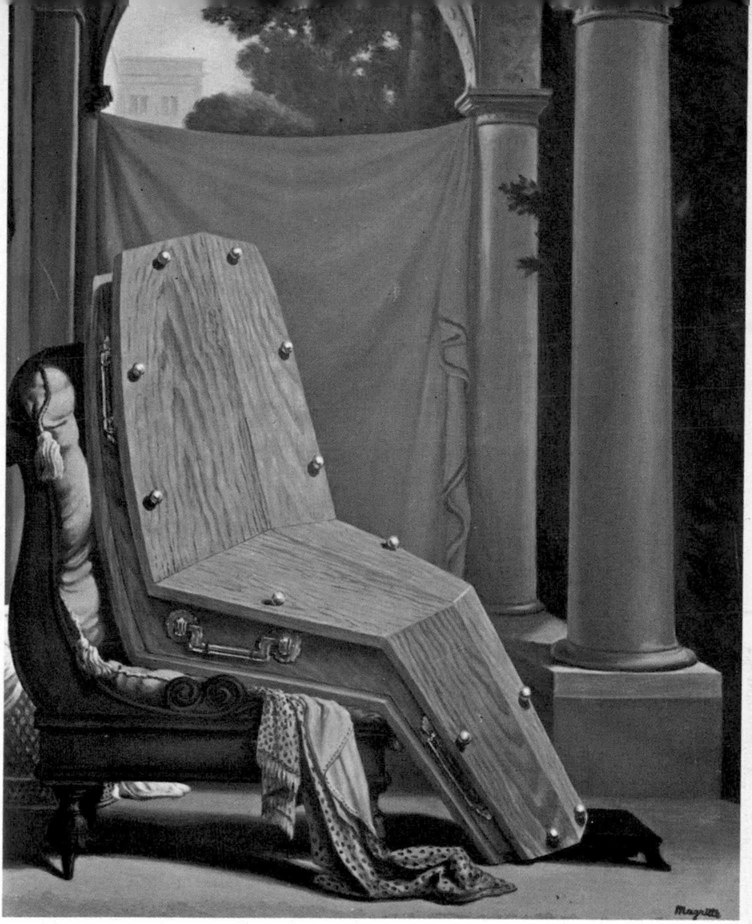

117. ***Perspective: Madame Récamier of Gérard,*** **by René Magritte**

forced to believe in what we see. He also indulged in surrealistic parody on occasion, with witty references to earlier paintings, sometimes spoofing them (Plate 117).

Magritte had a family history of suicides and nervous depressions. He studied at the Brussels Academy of Fine Arts and later took a job designing hideous wallpapers for Belgian living rooms. His free time he spent painting in his own way. After seeing the work of the Parisian surrealists, he moved to Paris and worked there from 1927 until 1930. Had his output during those years been greater, it is likely that he would have become the most distinguished of the surrealist painters.

Sculpture

TWO SCULPTORS made significant contributions to the surrealist movement. Having first studied in Strasbourg, Jean (Hans) Arp came into contact with Parisian art in 1904. His style was formed, however, by association with the Blaue Reiter group in Munich. He knew Apollinaire and his circle, and in 1916 Arp helped found the Dada movement in Zurich. He then worked with Max Ernst in Cologne. Arp did not concentrate his attention on sculpture until 1930. Even when he comes closest to representing the human figure, there is often a suggestion of organic vegetable form in his work (Plate 118). Arp's sculptures resemble one another in the subtle flow of one curved plane into another. His paintings are more surrealist in their suggestive forms than is his austere sculpture.

119. ***The Piazza,*** **by Alberto Giacometti**

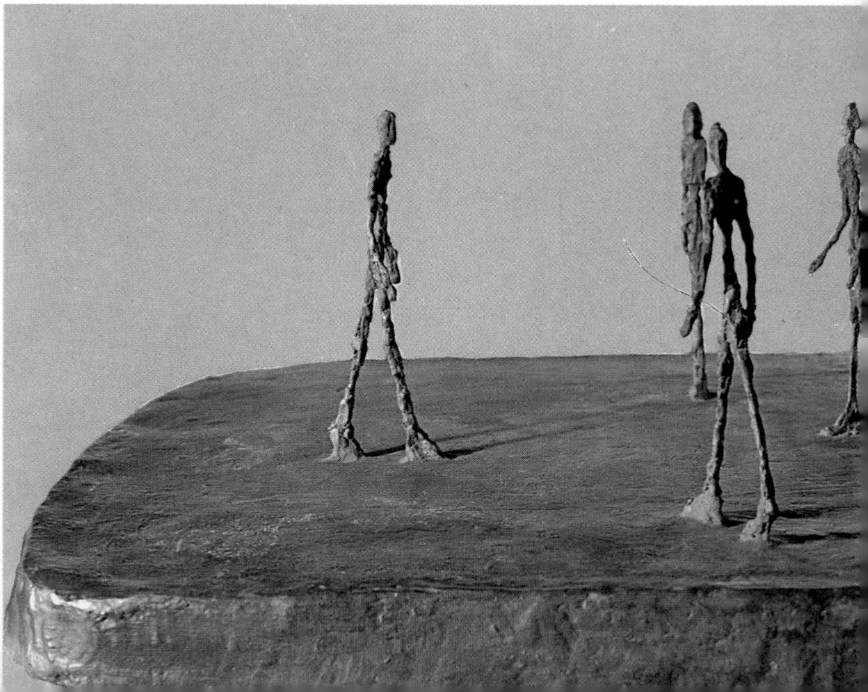

118. ***Human Concretion*****, by Jean Arp**

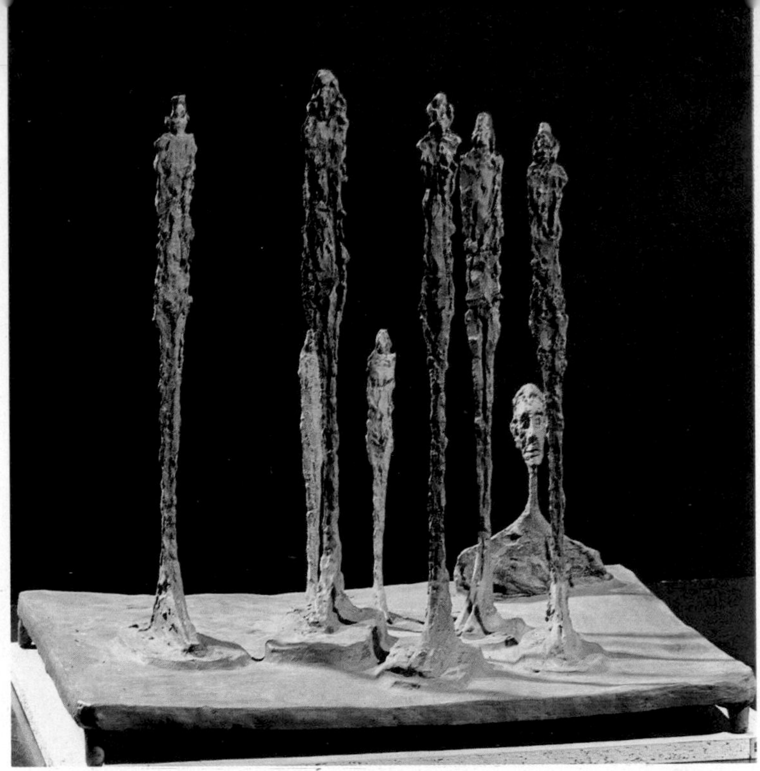

120. ***The Forest,*** **by Alberto Giacometti**

Alberto Giacometti (1901–1966), the son of a Swiss postimpressionist painter, came to artistic maturity in neither Dada nor surrealist circles. He had studied with the restrained and classical French sculptor Aristide Maillol (1861–1944). He did not first meet the surrealists until 1930. Although his association with them was brief, it did produce some authentically surrealist works.

In later years, Giacometti became increasingly preoccupied with themes of loneliness and isolation. *The Piazza* (Plate 119) is composed of five freestanding figures with no apparent interplay as individuals. Their elongated skeletal proportions are a Giacometti trademark. In *The Forest* (Plate 120) loneliness is grimly expressed by an isolated detailed face set in a forest of coldly silent semihuman figures.

Emile Antoine Bourdelle (1869–1929), like many sculptors, entered on his artistic career as a result of working in another craft during his youth. His father was a carpenter and cabinetmaker, and the young boy began by helping to carve the ornamental parts on sideboards made by his father. Bourdelle attended the Toulouse École des Beaux-Arts and subsequently went on to the École des Beaux-Arts in Paris. Finding the academic disciplines there too strict, however, he left after only a few months. In 1893 Bourdelle became an assistant to Rodin and remained with him for some fifteen years. Undoubtedly, to have been in continuous contact with the greatest sculptor of the age was very inspiring; yet it is possible that it also prevented Bourdelle from fully developing as a sculptor in his own right. His own personality might easily have become subdued by that of the greater man.

Bourdelle's monumental style was remarkable in its ability to treat great themes with power and control, even when he worked on a comparatively small scale. This power can be seen in his well-known *Hercules Aiming at the Stymphalian Birds* (Plate 121).

121. ***Hercules Aiming at the Stymphalian Birds,*** **by Emile Antoine Bourdelle**

122. *Venus with a Necklace,* **by Aristide Maillol**

123. *Paulette,* **by Charles Despiau**

By contrast, Aristide Maillol appears to have been interested in poise rather than in movement. His style varied little throughout his career, perhaps because he was already thirty-five when he became a sculptor. Earlier, he had pursued a career as a painter (he had been in contact with Gauguin and the Nabis in 1893), and then as a weaver of tapestries. All his work seems to be an attempt to avoid striking personality in an effort to be stately and monumental. His classical-looking nudes, which make up the greater part of his output, are somewhat static and generally over-life-size figures. Their ample bodies often have a certain thickness about them, like that of the *Venus with a Necklace* (Plate 122), and their placid faces are bare of human emotion.

There are similar objections to the sculpture of Charles Despiau (1874–1946). His masterpiece, the delicate *Paulette* (Plate 123), is not at all representative of his prevailing style. This work brought him to Rodin's attention, and Despiau became an assistant to the older sculptor for some time. In the end, however, Despiau seemed incapable of taking anything from his master, and he remained more or less academic and workmanlike in his own art.

Active also as a graphic artist and playwright, the German expressionist Ernst Barlach (1870–1938) is most noted for his compassionate sculpture. From his decorative Jugendstil (Art Nouveau) early style he went on, after contact with early Van Gogh and Millet paintings and with Russian folk religion, to develop an earthy yet monumental style that owed much to medieval metalcraft and woodcarving. He revived this latter, little-used technique, and its qualities influenced him even when he worked in stone. Through all his subjects, mostly beggars or other suffering figures, there runs a current of emotional mysticism that is in strange contrast to their robust proportions (Plate 124).

Another individual and gifted German sculptor of this era was Wilhelm Lehmbruck (1881–1919), whose academic beginnings and interest in Rodin's and Maillol's figure studies are evident in his later, more personal work. His career was ended prematurely when, at the age of thirty-eight and in ill health, he committed suicide. He was chiefly concerned with the nude figure, and in his best-known works—such as his meditative *Kneeling Woman*

124. ***Man Singing,*** **by Ernst Barlach**

of 1911 (Plate 125)—he exhibits a graceful style recalling qualities of both Art Nouveau and late Gothic sculpture.

The sculptor Constantin Brancusi (1876–1957) was by nature a man continually searching for the new. He left home at the age of eleven to explore the world, abandoning his father's Romanian farm for years of vagabondage, during which he wandered all over Eastern Europe. By 1898 he was back in Romania, at the Bucharest Art Academy, where he received several years of formal training in drawing and sculpture before arriving in Paris sometime after 1900. In that year the great dominating star of

125. *Kneeling Woman,* by Wilhelm Lehmbruck

126. ***The Maiastra,*** **by Constantin Brancusi**

the world of sculpture was, of course, Rodin. No young sculptor could fail to be influenced by him, and the heads that Brancusi produced in his first years in Paris were very like those of Rodin. But not only did the great sculptor influence the young—he had a tendency to swallow them whole. Sculptors such as Despiau who went to work for him as assistants never again produced any work with strong individual value and significance.

This was a fate that Brancusi avoided. An invitation to join Rodin at Meudon was refused. Brancusi quickly turned down the offer, an arrangement that would have made him financially comfortable. This he did not only through pride in his own independence, but through a deep realization that the whole method and the whole effect of Rodin's sculpture had to be abandoned. Brancusi disliked Rodin's smudged impressionistic modeling, his romanticism, and his frequent sentimental theatricality. This style had to be replaced by sculpture of clean outlines, in which there was nothing superfluous. The new sculpture must seem pared down rather than built up; it must be classical in its purity and restraint even if it was not classical in its forms.

Thus Brancusi took to producing such works as the *Maiastra* and *Sleeping Muse* (Plates 126, 127). The maiastra is a bird in a

127. *Sleeping Muse,* by Constantin Brancusi

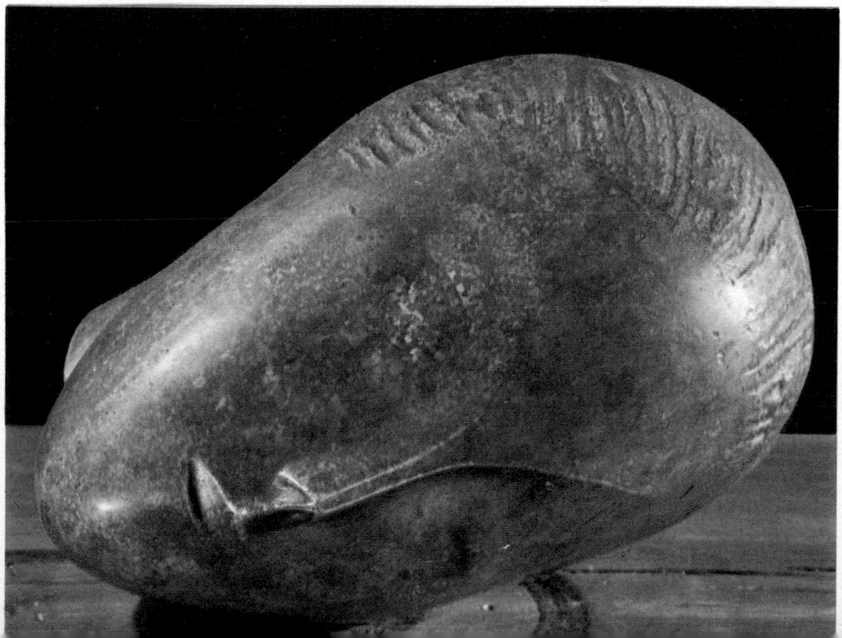

Romanian folktale which guides a lover through the forest to his imprisoned princess, thereby ensuring her release and their future happiness. The *Sleeping Muse* shares with several other of Brancusi's sculptures a tendency toward the elemental shape of the egg, revealing again his persistent concern with completely basic outlines.

Brancusi's early years in Paris were a time of stimulating contact with other artists. Modigliani especially was a close friend, and it was Brancusi who first encouraged him to try sculpture. Another friend was Henri Rousseau, for whose tomb Brancusi later carved a monumental pillar. He exhibited fairly frequently at the Salon d'Automne, sometimes with a startling effect on the public. Like so many other artists of his time, Brancusi was continually troubled by the public's failure to understand his work. He was involved for years in a lawsuit with the United States Customs Service, which refused to admit one of his works into America duty-free, as a work of art. They insisted that it was not a work of art, but merely a piece of polished metal and therefore taxable. It may have been incidents such as these which drove Brancusi into increasing isolation.

During World War I, Brancusi developed an interest in creating rough-hewn wood images like totem poles. Despite Brancusi's denials, these sculptures seem to have been inspired by primitive and exotic art. The wood carvings he created after the war, for example, *Adam and Eve* (Plate 128), became increasingly abstract. The totempole element in his work was developed to a surprising degree in his imposing *Endless Column,* which rises to a height of 98 feet. This daring and lovely sculpture, cast in gilded steel, was erected near his birthplace, at Târgu-Jiu, where it lends a disconcerting science-fiction touch to the wooded Carpathian landscape.

Antoine Pevsner (1886–1962) was born into a family of refinery engineers in Russia. This family background seems to have influenced strongly his direction as an artist. While his brother went to work in a copper refinery, Antoine attended the Kiev Academy of Fine Arts for several years. After arriving in Paris in 1913,

128. *Adam and Eve,* by Constantin Brancusi

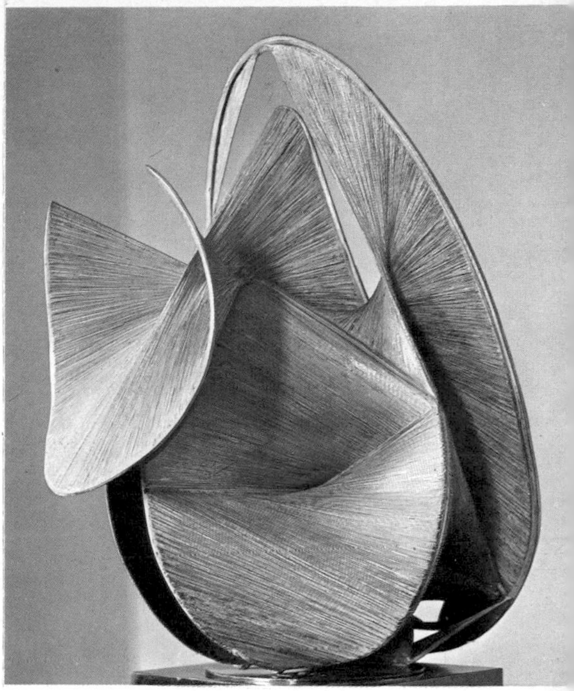

129. *Construction in an Egg,* by
Antoine Pevsner

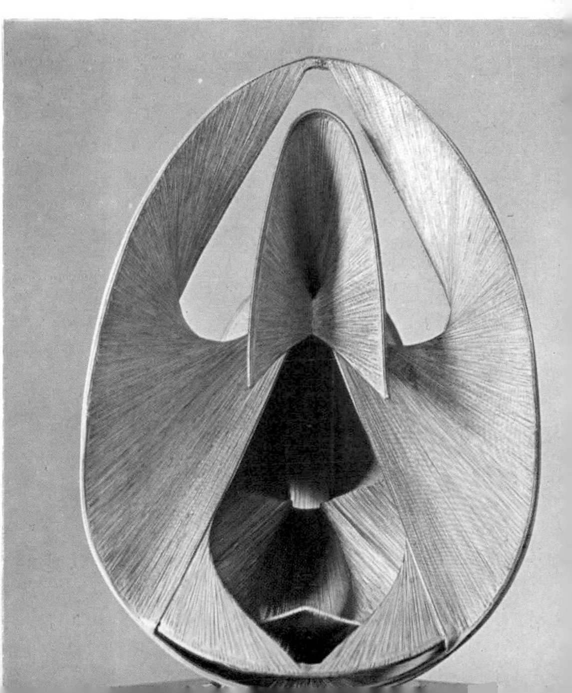

he became friendly with Modigliani and Archipenko and soon produced his first abstract painting.

From Paris, Pevsner went to Oslo, where he stayed from 1915 to 1917. This was to prove a most important period for him. In Oslo he was joined by his brother, Naum Gabo (1890–). While continuing to paint, Pevsner became more and more interested in his brother's sculpture and, finally, started to sculpt himself. The two brothers began to evolve a totally new kind of sculpture—new in that it began to use space itself as an integral part of the work of art (Plate 129), gradually leading to the abandonment of traditional principles of building sculpture out of compact masses. These revolutionary ideas were further developed during Pevsner's period as a teacher at the Moscow Higher Art and Technical School, where he was in continual contact with such artists as Kandinsky and Malevich.

In the wake of the Russian Revolution, both brothers signed the *Realist Manifesto,* which was printed by the revolutionary government in August, 1920, and posted all over Moscow. This document, which was of the greatest importance to modern sculpture, admirably summed up the guiding principles behind its development. The opening statement read, "If art is to be a reflection of real life, it should be based on two fundamental factors: space and time." Next, "Volume is not the only means of expressing space." The manifesto ended by declaring that "Art must cease to be imitative and must invent new forms."

About this time, the word "constructivist" was first used with reference to the brothers' work. Under the constructivist banner, Pevsner went to Berlin in 1922 with a government-sponsored exhibition of modern Russian art. He stayed in Germany for some months and then went on to Paris, where he finally made the decision to give up painting and devote himself to sculpture.

In 1924 the two brothers held a joint exhibition at the Galerie Percier in Paris, an exhibition that helped to make the direction their art was taking more definite and precise.

Pevsner's experiments with space and perspective led him to the use of transparent materials and to great freedom in combining open planes. Often his materials were varied: his *Portrait of*

130. ***Woman Combing Her Hair,*** **by Julio González**

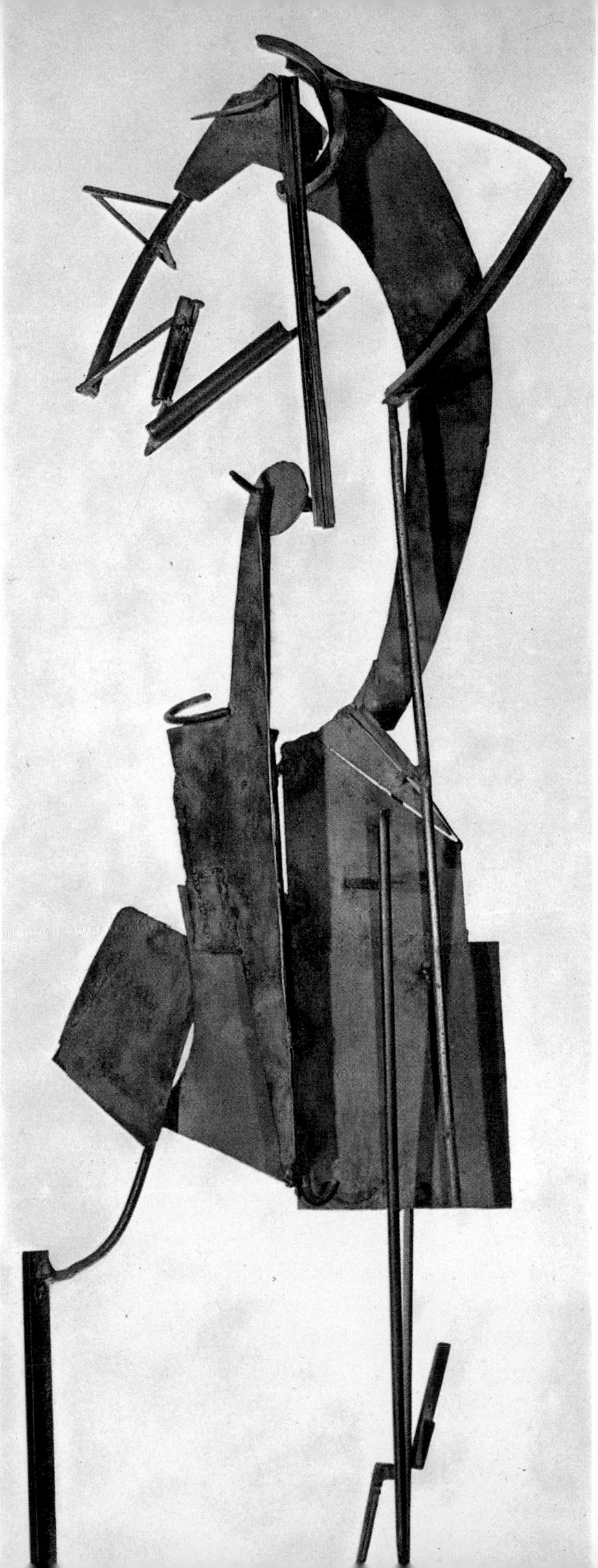

Marcel Duchamp (New Haven, Conn., Yale University Art Gallery), made of plates of zinc, copper, and celluloid, shows a clever use of contrast. In his later years, his work shows both clarity and purpose—a purposefulness and application that are also to be seen in the hard, craggy sculpture of the Spaniard Julio González (1876–1942).

González came from Barcelona; his father, a coppersmith, taught him to work in metal while he was studying at art school. But at this time of his life and in the years after 1900, when the whole family moved to Paris, González' main interest lay in painting. He produced heavy, somber canvases that were of little merit. When he finally took to sculpture, he worked, significantly, in iron. His metal sculpture is clearly the sculpture of a blacksmith.

Having learned acetylene welding at the Renault automobile factory, González went on to larger and more ambitious works. The iron was riveted and forged with a power that seems to surge through his compositions. In works such as the *Woman Combing Her Hair* (Plate 130) he was, like Pevsner, concerned with a new type of sculptural compostion. As he himself said, the aim was "to project space and draw in it, with the help of new mediums: to use this space and build with it, as if it were a newly discovered medium—that is my whole endeavor." In this, González achieved a great deal of success. Despite a life of poverty and unhappiness, which was largely spent in solitude, his output shows how right such other sculptors as Brancusi and Gargallo were to encourage and support him.

Pablo Gargallo (1881–1934) was another Spaniard, and one who also began at the art academy in Barcelona. In 1901 he shared a studio there with Picasso, and worked with him again when he went to Paris in 1906. The achievements of cubism in painting made Gargallo realize that sculpture lagged far behind. Although his style was basically traditional, Gargallo made certain advances in the art. Like González, he used iron. Although he was no true constructor of space, he did develop a technique, seen here in *Maternity* (Plate 131), which was new and which has since been influential in the work of other artists. The basic trick of this

131. *Maternity,* by Pablo Gargallo

technique was to translate convex planes into concave, and vice versa.

Gargallo helped his old friend Picasso when, in 1931, he decided to sculpt in metal. Gargallo was invited to Picasso's château at Boisgeloup to teach him the necessary techniques, and in the next year Picasso produced a large number of metal sculptures.

Two Eastern Europeans made individual contributions to the sculpture of the modern period. Ossip Zadkine (1890–1967) was sent from Russia, at the age of sixteen, to finish his education in, of all places, Sunderland, England. There he began to draw and sculpt at evening classes and then went to London, where he moved in literary and artistic circles. Far more decisive to his art was his move to Paris in 1909, where he immediately took to cubism. At this stage his work was more obviously cubist than that of any other sculptor; but these early works do not compare in quality with those of his maturity, such as the great Rotterdam monument (Plate 132), which commemorates with great force the destruction of Rotterdam by the Nazis.

Jacques Lipchitz arrived in Paris from his native Lithuania in the same year as Zadkine, and was similarly impressed with cubism. But his reaction to it was more timid, and his early attempts to translate the new language of painting into stone lacked power. It took him some time to find a personal style. He eventually achieved this by reducing his figures to their essential elements, producing at first a rather awkward effect. A later style, to which *Sacrifice II* and *Return of the Son* (Plates 133, 134) belong, has an assured sense of movement and an effective ability to construct in contours.

Still another significant sculptor who began his long career in this same period was Jacob Epstein (1880–1959). Born in New York of Polish Jewish parents, he worked first in a foundry; then, having emigrated, in 1902 he went to the École Nationale des Beaux-Arts and the Académie Julian in Paris. After this rather brief stay in Paris, he settled permanently in London, where his distinctive style shocked and at times enraged the British public from that time on. Eighteen statues commissioned by the British Medical Association first put him outside the pale of ordinary

Left: 132. ***Monument Commemorating the Destruction of Rotterdam,*** **by Ossip Zadkine**

Right: 133. ***Sacrifice II,*** **by Jacques Lipchitz**

middle-class opinion. This was the beginning of an alienation that troubled him all his life, although he never lacked commissions for his sculptures. Early in his career, probably in 1911, he was commissioned to do a statue for the tomb of Oscar Wilde, the famous English playwright and poet, in the Père La Chaise cemetery in Paris. This work already reveals the firm individuality of his sculptural imagination. Over the tomb he constructed a huge, heavy, sphinx-like figure of an angel. A very unusual angel

134. *Return of the Son,* by Jacques Lipchitz

it was, indeed, with an expression of puffy dissipation and heavy bags under its eyes. When the statue was set in position, the public and authorities howled in outrage. It was during the commotion of this period that Epstein first came into contact with Picasso, Modigliani, and Brancusi.

Later, Epstein modeled his famous *Visitation* (Plate 135). The extent to which public disapproval had worried Epstein can be gathered from his comment at the time: "This figure stands with folded hands, and expresses a humility so profound as to shame the beholder who comes to my sculpture expecting rhetoric or splendor of gesture. This work alone refutes all the charges of blatancy and self-advertisement leveled at me."

Epstein perhaps excelled as a religious sculptor. In this field he could effectively combine his intensely expressionistic style and his feeling for symbolic figures in a more traditional style. But his standard of portraiture was also very high, as seen in the bust *Selina* (Plate 136), which portrays his cleaning woman. Epstein's large-scale works are extremely stirring. These include his *War Memorial,* a powerful statement against war, and *St. Michael and the Devil,* a dramatic sculpture for Coventry Cathedral.

The British sculptor Henry Moore (1898–) is one of the major artists of our time, a superb craftsman and also a man of profound and complex vision. Born in Yorkshire, he first studied teaching and became an artist only after World War I. He had received some measure of recognition in England by 1928, when he was commissioned to make a relief for the St. James's underground (subway) station. At that time he usually worked by direct carving of stone or wood, as Michelangelo had felt before him. Moore believed that form lay concealed in the material, awaiting only the sculptor's revealing labor. Moore's respect and love for carving has provided the basis of his style. He is always aware of the solidity and heaviness of stone and of the grain and structure of wood, in working with those materials. After 1945, he began to work more in bronze. But the language of forms he had evolved over the years of carving by hand remained remarkably unchanged; only the surface texture was now different.

Left: 135. ***The Visitation,*** **by Sir Jacob Epstein**

Right: 136. ***Selina,*** **by Sir Jacob Epstein**

Throughout his life Moore has concentrated on a few themes, themes of extreme simplicity. These are mostly concerned with the human body—standing, sitting, or, more often, reclining (Plate 137). The single human figure has been a frequent subject in modern sculpture, often meant to express a feeling of tragic isolation. In Moore's work the single figure is quite different; it is vital, even in repose, with every contour emphasizing the life force (Plate 138). When Moore groups figures, they create an organic relationship.

After the reclining woman, the theme to which he most often returned was that of the mother and child. During World War II he did many drawings in the London bomb shelters. These drawings often featured shrouded women with children (Plate 139). When commissioned to make a Madonna and Child group after the war, he made a long series of preliminary studies for it. In these he incorporated a previous surrealist phase with the shelter drawings. The protective, enclosing mother figure of the finished *Madonna and Child* makes it one of his warmest, most renowned works.

Associated with Henry Moore in the group of British artists and architects known as Unit One, formed in 1933, was the sculptress Barbara Hepworth (1903–). The previous year she had also joined a circle of Parisian artists called Abstraction-Création, who practiced a style they designated *art concret.* This school of geometric abstraction was an outgrowth of the De Stijl movement and Russian constructivism, as transplanted to Paris. From an early naturalistic style, Barbara Hepworth has progressed toward a style of pure abstract shapes which reflects these international tendencies. Carving directly in wood and stone, she has shown in her severe pierced forms a special interest in the penetration of the sculptural mass by the surrounding space (Plate 140).

Another British sculptor who is of the same generation is Kenneth Armitage (1916–), who has produced many monumental cast-metal works. His philosophy of sculpture is perhaps best stated in his own words: "I like sculpture to look as if it had *happened,* and to express an idea as simply as possible. The moment when the work just sufficiently conveys the idea is the time also to finish, as further effort only neutralizes." His recurring theme has been these rudimentary figures, most often with several of them united in a single imposing bulk that has a suggestion of primitive religion or some primordial mystery about it (Plate 141).

137. ***Reclining Figure,*** **by Henry Moore**

Without doubt one of the most important American sculptors of this or any other period is Alexander Calder—engineer, illustrator, graphic artist, and inventor of the "mobile." Born in 1898, he first studied engineering, then drawing. At the age of twenty-eight, he went to Paris, where he made his first objects (sculpture is too misleading a term for these), which were a blend of cartoons and puppets. With these he put together a circus, with wire figures going round and round the ring, dancing and clowning. He

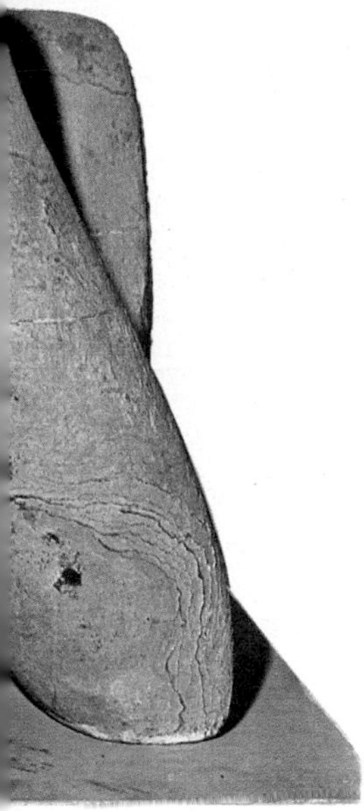

138. ***Warrior,*** **by Henry Moore**

used wire also to make a series of fascinating portraits that, when hung in a strong light, cast shadows of everchanging expressions on the wall. These simple animated caricatures set the course for his future experiments.

In 1931, he began to make much larger, abstract "sculptures" in which movement, though not yet actually present, was suggested by the forms. These elegant and lighthearted constructions, which Arp soon christened "stabiles," occupied Calder for some

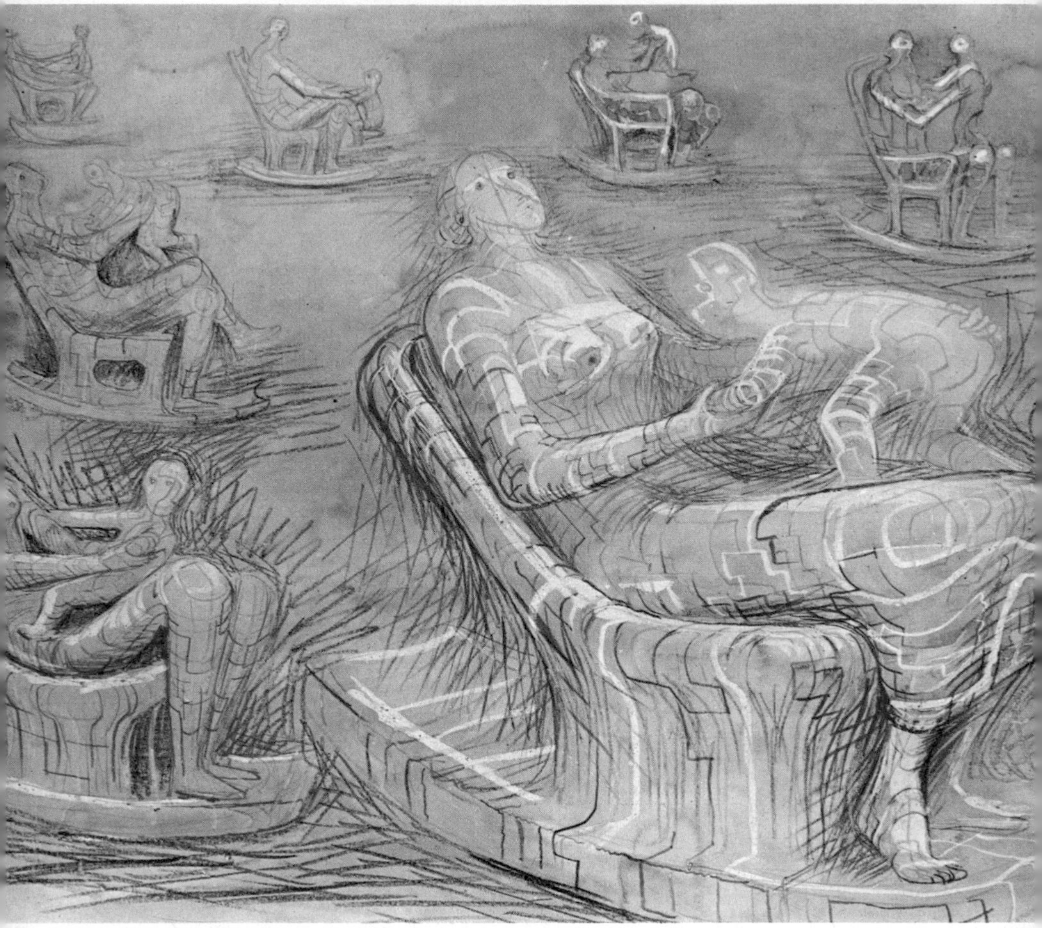

139. ***The Rocking Chair,*** **by Henry Moore**

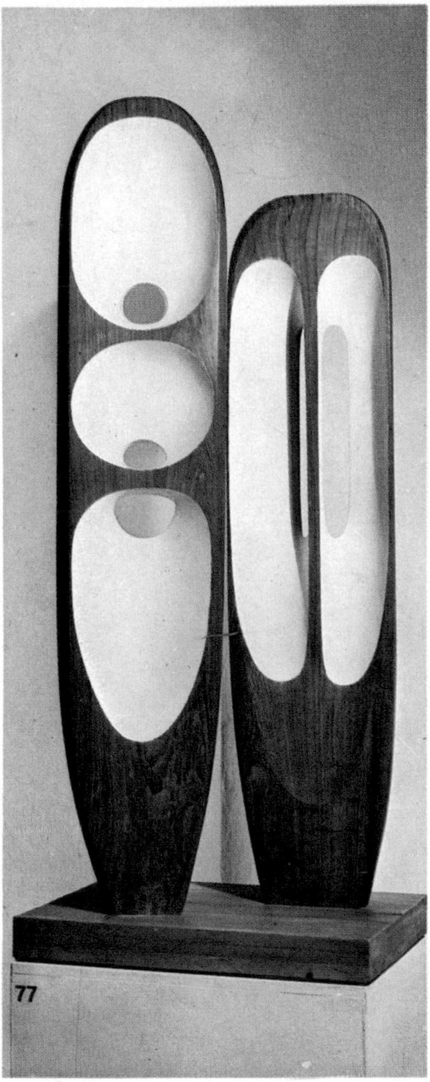

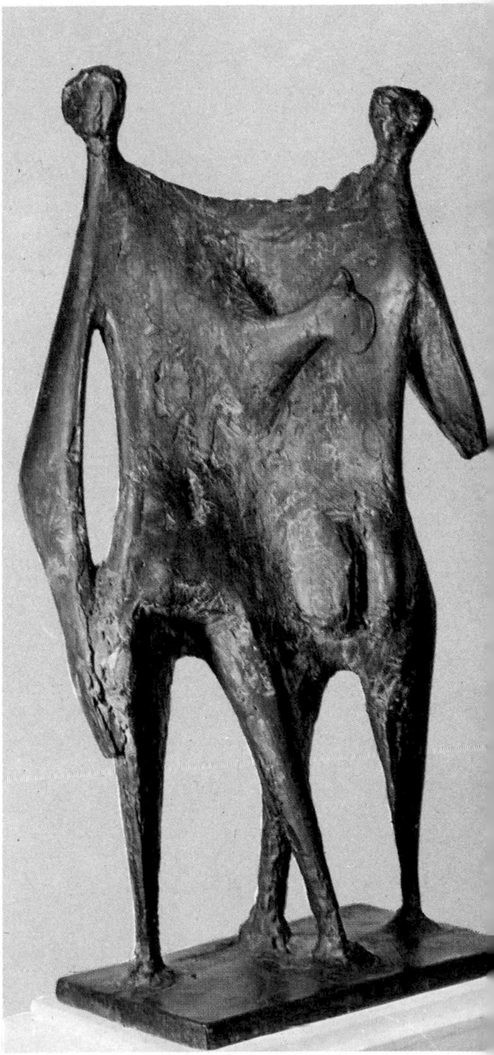

Left: 140. ***Two Figures (Menhir),*** **by Barbara Hepworth**

Right: 141. ***Two Standing Figures,*** **(1950), by Kenneth Armitage**

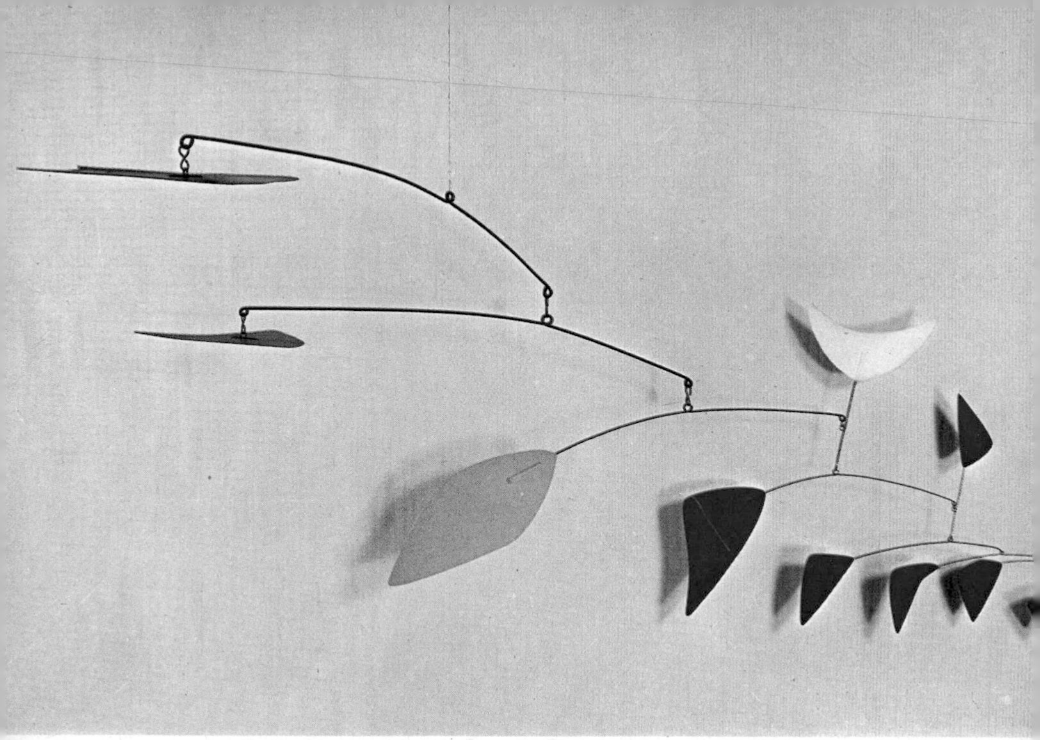

142. ***Mobile*, by Alexander Calder**

time. He then began to experiment with motorized versions, which the spectator could start and stop at will. But motors are an awkward artistic device, and Calder's major discovery, in 1932, was a way to create movement without such mechanical aids. Thus was born his distinctive art form, the "mobile."

Calder's mobiles, especially the early ones, look very simple. Their round or elegantly curved metal plates, which are either black or white or are painted in strong bright colors, hang on wires in flying formation in clusters and individually (Plate 142). When the slightest wind catches them, they bob and sway in diverting fashion, miraculously avoiding collisons by their carefully calculated arrangement. Frequently Calder placed them out of doors, in fields or in gardens, where like flowers and weathervanes they submit to the prevailing winds. Later he began to combine stable and mobile elements, using a framework to support the moving parts.

143. *The Great Spider,* by Alexander Calder

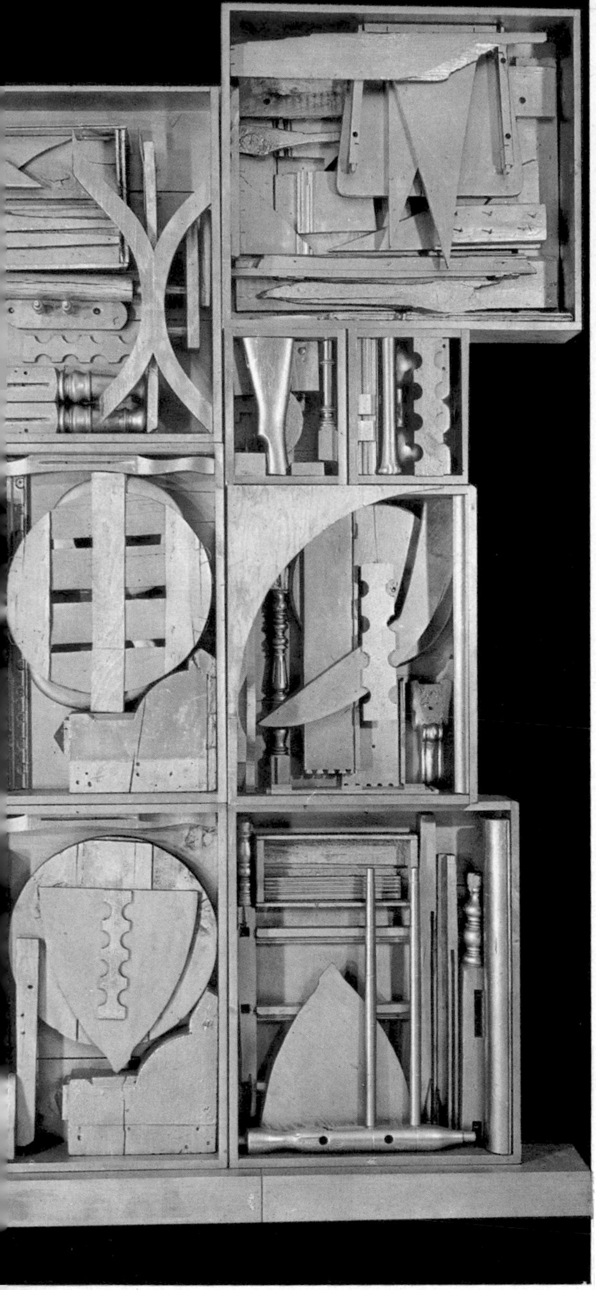

144. *Sun Image I,* **by Louise Nevelson**

Calder was able to absorb what he needed from European artists —Miró, Mondrian, and Léger were his friends—and still reject the European view of what art itself was. Like Jackson Pollock (1912–1956), another very influential American artist, he found a way of freeing form and color from their European bonds. The mobile was in part a triumph because it was so novel and had to be considered and looked at in an entirely new way. Few modern artistic devices have so liberated form—regarded as something fixed within definite limits, that is—and in this respect Calder's achievement is enormous. Since World War II, he has divided his time between America and Europe, continuing to make mobiles and stabiles (Plate 143), and doing book illustrations and stage design as well.

Like the varied welded-metal techniques that have been an important innovation in modern sculpture, mixed-media constructions and assemblages of "ready-made" or "found" objects have made significant contributions to the art. Belonging to this category, yet very different from the machine-like precision of earlier constructivist sculpture, is the work of the American artist Louise Nevelson (1900–). Her largescale constructions (Plate 144) are composed of a variety of hand-carved shapes and found items mounted in separate compartments that are stacked together and painted all over in a uniform color (black, white, or gold). Her chief material is wood, but on occasion she has used the Plexiglas of the constructivists in her crowded arrangements.

Born of a Japanese father and an American mother, sculptor Isamu Noguchi (1904–) studied art first in New York and then went to Paris, where he studied with Constantin Brancusi in 1927–1928. In works such as his over-life-size marble *Kouros* ("Youth", Plate 145), the influence of his master's pure, rigorously simplified forms is apparent, but in a highly personal and refined Oriental manner. Noguchi has been active also as a theatrical designer, notably for the modern dance productions of the Martha Graham troupe. Further evidence of his great versatility may be found in his furniture and lamp designs, his work as a landscape architect, and his terracotta pieces, produced after he had traveled to Japan to study ceramic art.

145. *Kouros,* by Isamu Noguchi

146. ***Sea Sentinel,*** **by Theodore Roszak**

147. ***Artist and Model,*** **by Giacomo Manzù**

Noteworthy among modern sculptors who work with welded metals, in the tradition of González and Gargallo, is the American Theodore Roszak (1907–). Accomplished in the use of blacksmith's tools and the acetylene torch, he devised a unique and complicated method of imposing surfaces of bronze and brass onto a solid steel base. His barbed organic shapes, agitated yet monumental in appearance, suggest some kind of fantastic marine or vegetable life (Plate 146).

Among the most important sculptors in Italy following World War II have been Giacomo Manzù (1908–) and Marino Marini (1901–).

In certain of his works, Manzù reveals himself as a very intellectual humorist in the uses of art. Besides being a masterful sculptor in a fairly traditional manner, he has made brilliant contributions to the discussion of what art is and what its proper subjects should be. During World War II he took shelter in the mountains of Italy, where he worked on, among other things, a series of Crucifixion scenes in which German soldiers played the part of the executioners. In 1949 he was chosen to make the fifth bronze door for St. Peter's in Rome, and has since done many commissions for churches as well as pursued his own highly personal experiments.

Manzù's series of seated and standing figures of cardinals has brought him international fame. He has also done much work in the form of high-relief panels (Plate 147), which are very strongly pictorial in their placement of almost fully rounded figures against a plain background. These somehow bring to mind the great Italian medieval and Renaissance sculpted door panels, or even Roman classical reliefs.

Marino Marini has enjoyed great popularity as well as critical recognition. His most successful and widely known efforts are his numerous horse-and-rider sculpture groups, which range from calmly monumental to highly abstract treatments of the theme (Plate 148). He has also been extremely productive both as a painter and as a lithographer.

A third contemporary Italian sculptor of prominence is Mirko (family name, Basaldella; 1910–). His magical totemlike forms and finely engraved surface decoration call to mind the qualities of ancient Chinese ritual bronzes.

148. *Horse and Rider,* by Marino Marini

European Painting: Between the Wars and After

GERMAN PATRIOTISM and German pride, so strong and assured before World War I, seemed to go up in smoke in the aftermath of the 1918 armistice. The artistic life of postwar Germany left its bitter record in the work of painters loosely grouped in a movement known as the "Neue Sachlichkeit" ("New Objectivity"). These painters were not interested, as were many artists elsewhere in Europe, in the new language of abstraction. They expressed their cynical views of official and social corruption in a war-tired country with a bitter, intensely felt realism.

George Grosz (1893–1959) was one of the originators of the Neue Sachlichkeit trend. His powerful satire, with its contempt for all tradition and social convention, was a reflection of his high-strung and violent personality.

Grosz started his career as an effectively vicious political cartoonist for the satirical magazines of his day. He became associated with the Dada movement in Berlin toward the end of World War I and produced savage pamphlets and paintings expressing his hatred of modern urban life. *The Funeral of the Poet Panizza* (Plate 149), for example, is a stinging social statement. The extreme distortions of perspective, the jumbled forms, the coffin, the skeleton, and the cookie-faced priest are all combined in an episode of social outrage. Grosz felt that an artist "should know how to present the outer appearance of things together with their inner content." He definitely succeeded in this aim. Following the war, he mercilessly chronicled the prevailing evils of Germany, in some of the finest and fiercest pictorial satire ever created (Plate 150).

While Grosz may have set the general tone of German painting after the war, that country's most mature and noteworthy artist

149. *The Funeral of the Poet Panizza,* **by George Grosz**

was Max Beckmann (1884–1950), who possessed enough individuality and personal integrity to cut a path of his own through these chaotic years. A product of the conservative Weimar Academy of Art, Beckman began his artistic career as a fairly typical expressionist. Following the example of Grosz, Beckmann went through a deliberately gruesome stage in which he painted scenes of frightening cruelty. He emerged from this phase and, learning from cubism, began to compose his pictures in a firmer, more disciplined manner. It was not until 1925, however, that he came to full maturity as a painter, with a distinct contribution of his own.

Beckmann's later paintings, which often deal with the same themes as his earlier ones and have the same gloomy outlook, seem nevertheless calmer and more rooted in the artist's experience of the world (Plate 151). Beckmann then turned to great mythological and Biblical scenes, as in his *Perseus Triptych* (a triptych is a set of three related panel paintings). *The Departure* (Plate 152), though it seems intended to illustrate some ancient legend, also expresses feelings of exile and anxiety that were current in the Europe of the 1930's.

150. ***Metropolis,*** **by George Grosz**

151. ***Two Women,*** **by Max Beckmann**

Otto Dix (1891–), unlike Beckmann in his later career, appears never to have recovered spiritually from the suffering and pain he had seen and undergone himself in trench warfare, nor from witnessing the misery of gassed and wounded soldiers. Because of their intensity, his feelings were difficult to communicate in terms of traditional painting. At first he experimented with making fantastic Dada collages out of ugly materials. These

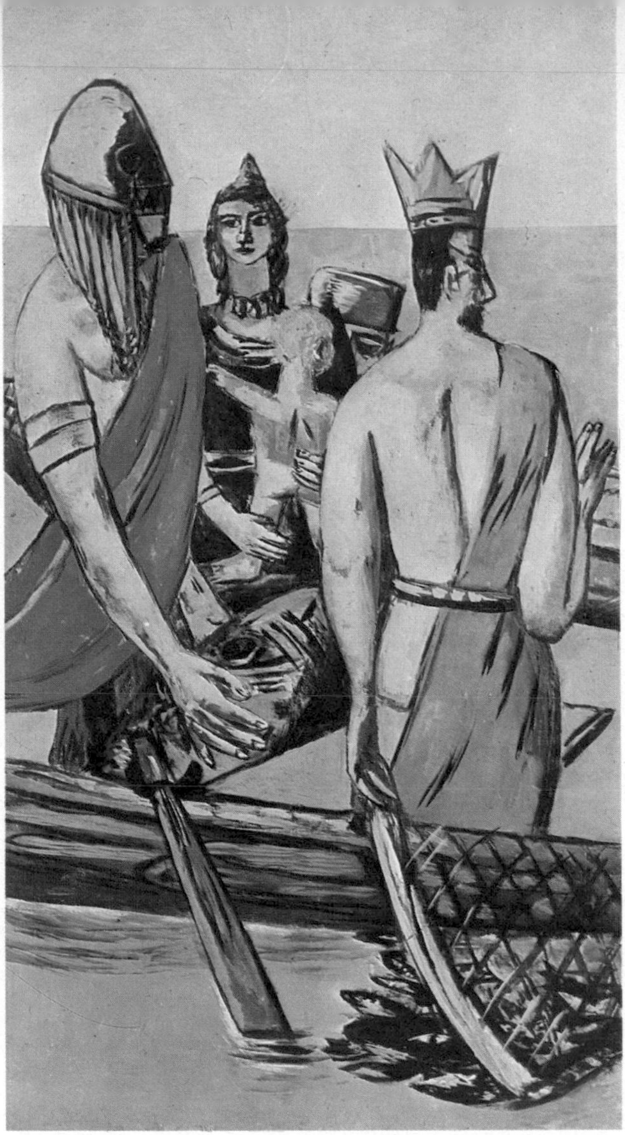

152. ***The Departure,*** **by Max Beckmann**

works are, as they were meant to be, shocking. He was still more successful when he turned to painting repulsive subjects such as corpse-littered yards in photographic detail.

This hard, expressive realism of the postwar years was practiced in other countries as well. In Belgium, Constant Permeke (1886–1952) painted large, simplified figures of miners and

153. ***The Sailor Brothers,*** **by Constant Permeke**

peasants. Vigorously and dramatically presented, these are generally rendered in dark, burnt-looking colors. The drawing of the faces is quite original and manages to capture character (Plate 153). These massive figures are vaguely similar to the sturdy people in the works of the French painter Marcel Gromaire (1892–), as seen in *The Lottery* (Plate 154).

154. *The Lottery,* **by Marcel Gromaire**

155. *The Suburb,* **by Mario Sironi**

A similar movement toward realism took place in Italy after World War I. This direction was most clearly seen in the magazine *Valori Plastici* ("Plastic Values"), the most influential publication concerning modern Italian painting. In particular, this magazine encouraged a return to the artistic forms of the great Italian tradition.

The painters who accepted the premises of *Valori Plastici* all too often produced monotonous uninspired paintings. But a few of them—Mario Sironi (1885–1961), in particular—managed to combine freshness with traditional qualities. In 1920, Sironi began a notable series of paintings depicting the dreary outskirts of industrial cities (Plate 155). Railway sidings, factories, and warehouses, painted in a limited range of browns, greenish grays, and dull whites, are combined in designs that have an unconventional strength.

This "general movement of realism was known as "Novecento Italiano" ("Italian Twentieth Century"). The first exhibit of Novecento Italiano in 1926 made it quite obvious that one of the most talented of the group's members was Filippo de Pisis (1896–1956). De Pisis experimented with a number of modern styles, but none seemed to suit his own poetic and delicate temperament. He finally found what he was looking for on a trip to Paris in 1926. It was not the modern movement that excited him, but the shimmering color of the impressionists. From these painters he derived the gentle, lovely style to be seen in *Peonies* (Plate 156).

The French painter Alfred Manessier (1911–   ) was one of the founding members of a group of abstract artists called "Peintres de tradition française" ("Painters in the French tradition"), which began its activity in 1941. Rather than the severe geometry of *art concret* and Purism, however, they chose to use freer abstract shapes in a style drawn from earlier cubist and even impressionist innovations in space and color—with a particular debt to Picasso. Characteristic of their art was its bright vibrant color, which added to the expressive power of the symbolic forms they created (Plate 157).

Born in St. Petersburg, Russia, Nicolas de Staël (1914–1955) was one of those twentieth-century artists who are loosely designated

156. ***Peonies,*** **by Filippo de Pisis**

as members of the "school of Paris." Rather than representing a single unified style, this name has been given to numerous artists, both French and foreign, who have worked in Paris over several generations and who have displayed varying—though mostly abstract—stylistic tendencies. De Staël himself might be called one of the "second generation" of the school of Paris. To the Belgian theorist and art historian Michel Seuphor, he once identified his ideals as "Braque, Cézanne, and Matisse, and nobody else—nobody." The inspiration of these, one might say, "classic" masters of the modern movement is apparent in De Staël's bright-

157. ***Evening Offering,*** **by Alfred Manessier**

159. ***The Financial and Economic System,*** **by Georges Mathieu**

hued yet strongly architectural abstractions (Plate 158). In the last few years before his suicide at Antibes, he was again moving toward a more representational style and was also abandoning his brilliant palette in favor of more somber colors.

As in the United States, one of the important post-World War II trends in France has been the type of painting known as "abstract expressionism" or, more appropriately, "action painting." The terms used to describe the style in France are *art informel* and "tachism"—the latter being derived from the French word for "blot" or "stain." Those who paint in this style place strong emphasis on accidental effects that arise in the course of painting. In these impulsive, "unplanned" works, there is a stress on the

158. ***Le Lavandou,*** **by Nicolas de Staël**

very process or act of painting and whatever chance visual results it may lead to. (One should not, however, underestimate the amount of artistic control and choice involved in such "accidents.") Further, these artists determined to be completely "uninhibited by the past."

One of the most notable exponents of tachism is Georges Mathieu (1921–), who has demonstrated its wonderful and unpredictable possibilities by creating at least one of these action paintings extemporaneously before an audience. Both he and his countryman Pierre Soulages (1919–) borrow heavily from Oriental ideograms for compositions rendered in a deliberately limited range of colors (Plates 159, 160).

A French artist whose work very often resembles the art of children or that of the mentally disturbed is Jean Dubuffet (1901–), who has also spent time working in the United States. Originally a wine merchant and an occasional painter, Dubuffet has

160. ***February 9*****, by Pierre Soulages**

dedicated himself fully to art since 1942. In its comment on modern times, his *art brut* ("raw art") is a witty, sometimes bitter continuation of the surrealist and Dada spirit. In a style that combines thick-layered patches of brushwork with the slashing lines of caricature, there are also suggestions of primitive and barbarian art (Plate 161).

Dubuffet's pictures resemble nothing so much as the walls of dilapidated buildings, pitted and scratched, covered with dirt, and scribbled all over. His attack on traditional values is at its best when he is being ironical. He paints cows or portraits in a childish manner that dignifies the cows and makes his portraits seem like animals. Earlier in his career Dubuffet used to paint a grotesque caricature first and only later add someone's name as a title. Resemblance to any living person might well have caused offense! This is clearly illustrated in his *Portrait of Edith Boissonnas* (Plate 162).

161. ***Rue Brise Elan*, by Jean Dubuffet**

162. ***Portrait of Edith Boissonnas,*** **by Jean Dubuffet**

Three twentieth-century British painters have gained significant international reputations and influence: Francis Bacon (1910–), Graham Sutherland (1903–), and Ben Nicholson (1894–).

Both Bacon and Sutherland are loosely associated with a trend sometimes known as the "new realism," which has its roots in past English painting. Their work, clearly in the line of earlier visionary painters, often has strong literary allusions. Their personal outlook has taken quite different directions, however. In a style that has shown tinges of surrealism, metaphysical painting, and even *art informel,* Bacon has presented an essentially desperate and bleak view of the world (Plate 163). The pitiable condition of mankind that he observes produces feelings of helplessness and dread in the viewer.

Sutherland instead, perhaps as a result of his conversion to Catholicism, strikes a more affirmative note. He studied and first became known for engraving in the 1920's and 1930's. After a

163. ***Portrait of Van Gogh,*** **by Francis Bacon**

164. ***Thorn Trees,*** **by Graham Sutherland**

brief foray into surrealism, Sutherland arrived at the style for which he is best known in the years during and after World War II. Based on nature, the spiky forms characteristic of his mature semiabstract style (Plate 164) also show the significant impression made upon him by Picasso's *Guernica.* In certain of his works, Sutherland has also given evidence of his close friendship with Francis Bacon. He generally chooses to depict strange or ghostly aspects of nature, natural features that are made to suggest disturbing human forms. Following World War II, he did a series of religious paintings that are powerful and vigorously modern within their basically representational style. Sutherland has also done some harsh and unconventional, yet realistic, portraits of famous sitters such as Winston Churchill and Somerset Maugham.

Painting: The American Scene

IN THE first years of the twentieth century, painting in the United States was largely dominated by impressionist and postimpressionist styles. But the quiet course of American painting was violently disturbed by three major exhibitions: a showing of Matisse in 1908, of Picasso in 1911, and, most important, of a large group of recent (and some nineteenth-century) European paintings in several American cities in 1913. This last was the famous Armory Show. Intended originally as an exhibit of contemporary American art, the show was stolen by the radically new European styles of cubism, expressionism, Fauvism, and Orphism. By comparison the American painters shown seemed unadventurous and hopelessly out-of-date.[1] The reaction of the general public ranged from astonishment to outrage, and the publicity—or more aptly, notoriety—attending the exhibition was enormous. In its aftermath, American art would never again be the same.

The American artist John Sloan (1871–1951) had been painting for many years before the Armory Show. He was a member of "The Eight," a group of artists who in 1908, fed up with smothering academic traditions, exhibited their "radical" realist paintings together.[2] They were among the first to take the ordinary street life of New York as a subject for painting, and their art was jeeringly nicknamed the "Ash Can school."

[1] Among the older mid- and late-nineteenth-century masters exhibited were Cézanne, Corot, Courbet, Daumier, Delacroix, Degas, Gauguin, Goya, Ingres, Manet, Monet, Munch, Pissarro, Puvis de Chavannes, Redon, Renoir, Seurat, Sisley, Toulouse-Lautrec, and Van Gogh.

More recent modern European artists shown included Archipenko, Bonnard, Brancusi, Braque, Delaunay, Derain, Duchamp, Dufy, Epstein, Kandinsky, Kirchner, La Fresnaye, Léger, Lehmbruck, Maillol, Marquet, Matisse, Pascin, Picabia, Picasso, Rodin, Rouault, Henri Rousseau, Villon, and Vuillard. (The selection of Matisse and Picasso works was particularly generous. However, the artist deliberately shown to the most extensive and greatest advantage was Odilon Redon.)

165. *Haymarket,* by John Sloan

Sloan had been strongly influenced by Robert Henri (1865–1929), the leader of the group and the son of a fugitive from a Nebraska gunfight. Unlike Henri, Sloan quickly perceived that the work of Matisse, Brancusi, Kandinsky, and Duchamp held great lessons for American art. As he himself recalled, "I consciously began to be aware of the techniques of art. While I have made no abstract paintings, I have absorbed a great deal from the world of the ultra-modern." Therefore, although his *Haymarket* (Plate 165) reveals Sloan as a typical member of "The Eight," his paintings after the Armory Show became clearer in composition, and their structure obviously owed a great deal to the European examples.

George Bellows (1882–1925) was another painter who began with Robert Henri in New York, in 1904. His exceptional talent

[2] Besides Sloan and Robert Henri, the other members of "The Eight"—all noteworthy names in American art—were: George Luks (1867–1933), William J. Glackens (1870–1938), Everett Shinn (1873–1953), Arthur B. Davies (1862–1928), Maurice Prendergast (1859–1924), and Ernest Lawson (1873–1939).

166. ***The Solitary Tenement,* by George Bellows**

soon led to membership in the National Academy, and it was at this time that he, like Sloan, turned to a more structured kind of painting. In his case the example came from Jay Hambidge (1867–1924), who formulated the theory of "dynamic symmetry," a system of geometry underlying the main lines of the painting. Bellows followed Hambidge's theories of proportion and proclaimed that "there are no successful pictures without a geometric basis." Bellows became an extremely popular painter, especially for his sporting scenes. (He once thought of becoming a professional baseball player.) Basically a traditionalist, however, Bellows himself did little to advance the course of painting in America through his work (Plate 166).

This progress was accomplished by two artists, Joseph Stella (1880–1946) and John Marin (1870–1953), who wanted to readjust American traditions and bring them in line with contemporary developments in France and Italy.

Stella, an Italian immigrant, entered serious art after being trained as a commercial artist and illustrator for popular journals in New York. While working for *The Survey,* on a commission to

167. ***Brooklyn Bridge, Variations on an old theme,*** **1939 by Joseph Stella**

168. ***Quoddy Head, Maine Coast,*** **by John Marin**

draw steel mills, he decided that modern industrial subjects should form the subject matter of his art. He went back to Europe for four years (1908–1912), and there fully absorbed French cubism and the Orphism of Robert Delaunay. The interlocking circular motion of Orphism can be seen in his *Brooklyn Bridge* (Plate 167) and in other American landscapes of the period. But it was the urgent speed of American urban life that really excited him, and in painting this he was even more influenced by futurism. "I was thrilled," he said, "to find America so rich with so many new motives [motifs] to be translated into a new art. Steel and electricity had created a new world."

John Marin, on the other hand, was less moved by modern city life than by the American landscape. Working largely in watercolor, he made delicate renderings of the natural world, which seem at first to owe a great deal to impressionism; these are more

169. ***American Gothic*, by Grant Wood**

170. ***House of Mystery*, by Charles Burchfield**

valuable, as works of art, than are his city scenes. Marin's free, sketchy technique became more and more abstract in his later years. Landscapes such as *Quoddy Head, Maine Coast* (Plate 168) were translated in terms of pure paint.

A group of regional painters, led by Thomas Hart Benton (1889–), Charles Burchfield (1893–1967), John Steuart Curry (1897–1946), and Grant Wood (1892–1942), devoted themselves to the presentation of American rural life. Grant Wood was in many ways typical of all of them. A trained artist, he chose to paint in a deliberate, self-consciously primitive style, continuing the early American tradition of sharp outlines and a hard, precise brushstroke. This was intensified after his visits to Flanders and Germany, where he developed his appreciation of the technique of Flemish and German late Gothic and early Renaissance painters. Wood's minute detail often has a toylike quality, and the background of his *American Gothic* (Plate 169) reminds one that he once earned his living as a maker of miniature model houses.

Charles Burchfield was another regionalist who chose to paint the country he knew and loved. His art combines two important qualities: a feeling for the essential spirit of a particular landscape and an involvement with American history. *November Evening,* one of his finest works, is a poetic recollection of the days of Midwest pioneering. In its attention to domestic detail and sensitive treatment of woodwork and stone, Burchfield's *House of Mystery* (Plate 170) shows a certain resemblance to a painting by Edward Hopper (1882–1967), *House on the River Pamet.*

More characteristic of Hopper's work, however, is his *Night Café* (Plate 171), one of many rather melancholy paintings that arose from his personal experience with the loneliness of cities. Also trained by Robert Henri, Hopper was included in the Armory Show; afterward he did not change his style to any great extent but continued to paint in much the same way and with the same moody, slightly critical outlook. His paintings were created in his head, never from sketches or models.

Two American painters with a wholehearted devotion to the cause of abstract painting were Arthur G. Dove (1880–1946) and Stuart Davis (1894–1967). Dove painted the first American ab-

stracts. Though he always started from the natural appearance of things, he produced works, such as *Flour Mill Abstraction* (Plate 172), with no clear representational content.

Stuart Davis has the distinction of having introduced to American painting the areas of pop culture—advertising, jazz, the lights of Broadway—that have since become a major concern of the arts. Just as Dove foretells the abstract expressionism of the 1940's and 1950's, so too Davis sets a precedent for the Pop artists of the 1960's in his work (Plate 173).

"I took my place in the 1930's as part of the general uprising of social consciousness in art and literature," recollected the social realist Jack Levine (1915–). Like many other painters of the

171. ***Night Café,*** **by Edward Hopper**

time, he was opposed alike to abstract art and to surrealism. Levine felt that he should try to "do something for the world." His paintings, lively and free in handling, expose corruption in American life with great satiric force (Plate 174).

Philip Evergood (1901–) has used a sharper line and simpler compositions, often with an element of fantasy, to make similar social statements. *Lily and the Sparrows* (Plate 175) is a surrealistic, personal work; in other, more public-minded paintings, he has sternly condemned such social ills as race prejudice and the poverty of American blacks in the midst of general affluence.

Another fine painter of protest is Ben Shahn (1898–1969). The

172. *Flour Mill Abstraction,* **by Arthur G. Dove**

173. *The Paris Bit,* **by Stuart Davis**

174. *Welcome Home!,* **by Jack Levine**

LINES THICKEN
HOTEL
'28
PAD
EAU

175. ***Lily and the Sparrows,*** **by Philip Evergood**

son of Lithuanian Jewish parents, he arrived in the United States as an immigrant child. Raised in one of the poorest sections of Brooklyn, he was a lithographer's apprentice by day and studied at night classes after work. These classes eventually led him to New York University, and after that he made trips to France, Italy, Spain, and North Africa. Acutely conscious of developments in European painting, he felt uneasy about adapting them to his own style. An important decision was taken when he decided to give up all such attempts at changing his already formed artistic character. '"Here I am,' I said to myself, 'thirty-two years old, the son of a carpenter. I like stories and people. The French School is not for me.'"

It was at this stage that Shahn turned to social themes and began his famous series depicting the trial of Sacco and Vanzetti (Plate 176), two Italian anarchists who had been convicted of murder on an obviously trumped-up charge. The verdict, the result of anti-communist hysteria, was an insult to American justice and free-

176. ***The Passion of Sacco and Vanzetti,*** **by Ben Shahn**

dom. Horrified and angry, Shahn was so deeply moved that he felt, "Here I was living through another crucifixion. Here was something to paint!" In seven months he produced twenty-three gouache (tempera) paintings that show both restraint and dignity in their approach to the trial and ultimate execution. His somber theme is treated with compassion and frankness.

The Sacco and Vanzetti paintings, exhibited in New York, were much admired by the Mexican artist Diego Rivera, then at work on his murals for Rockefeller Center. Rivera hired Shahn as an assistant, and Shahn's first mural commission, at a housing development for garment workers where he himself lived, shows unmistakable signs of Rivera's influence. Shahn's deep social sense mirrored many aspects of American life; it was not a distorting mirror, but rather a sharply critical one. Another series of his gouache paintings, which dealt with the persecuted trade unionist Tom Mooney, showed livelier color and a more complicated technique.

Among Americans who were most directly affected by contact with surrealism, Arshile Gorky (1904–1948) is an outstanding example. Most influenced at first by Picasso and Miró, he explored their discoveries and made them his own, always adding something personal to them. He eventually developed his own symbolic "language." His subdued color comes second to the drawing, which presents a succession of active areas and quiet spots. The viewer is left to use his imagination freely in interpreting Gorky's works. In *Betrothal II* (Plate 177) the drawing at various points suggests people, plants, and animals; but the ceremony in which these forms are engaged remains a puzzle.

Gorky was also affected by the Chilean painter Matta (Roberto Sebastian Matta Echaurren; 1912–   ), who had emigrated to France but also worked in the United States. The importance of Matta, who had formerly studied architecture with Le Corbusier in the 1930's, lies in the scale and complexity of his fantastic, abstract surrealist pictures and the way these draw the spectator into their space. Once the artist himself wrote, "What does it Matta if Matter is mad as a Hatta?" [Sic] The over-all effect of his pictures is that of some insane vision—as seen, for instance, in

177. *Betrothal II,* by Arshile Gorky

the half-insect, half-machine figures in *Removal of the Cards* (Plate 178).

The influence of surrealism on American artists was apparent in diverse ways. Among others so influenced were the group called "magic realists," exemplified in the paintings of George Tooker (1920–   ). Their painstakingly detailed realism was so strange in its uniformly sharp focus and its dreamlike atmosphere that it took on surrealistic character. This curious effect derived from

 the magic realists' traits of unnaturally smooth surfaces, hypnotic

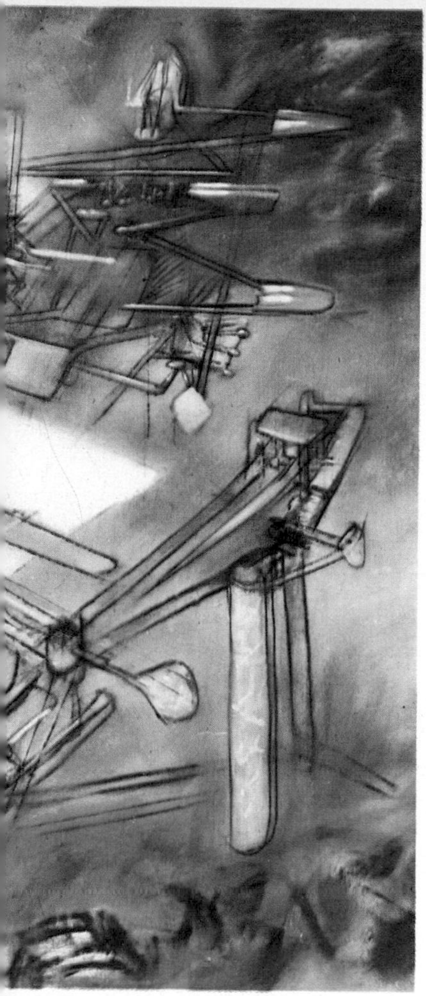

178. ***Removal of the Cards,*** **by Roberto Matta (Echaurren)**

expressions, and a kind of suspended movement throughout (Plate 179).

Throughout the 1930's and 1940's, the American art world was significantly affected by the arrival of European artists, many of them with already established reputations. Fleeing from a hostile political climate, they continued their careers in North America, enriching the artistic scene and often, in turn, being influenced by their new homeland. Among these was the painter Hans Hofmann (1880–1966), who came from Germany in 1930.

179. ***The Waiting Room,*** **by George Tooker**

Like other noted European emigrés, such as Archipenko and Moholy-Nagy, Hofmann was influential as a master teacher as well as a working artist. He became one of the prime forces in the development of abstract trends in the United States. During the early part of his career, in Germany, he had been in contact with Kandinsky and had worked in an expressionist style. Gradually his expressionism became more abstract, and his late works are characterized by the vigorous brushwork and strong color of

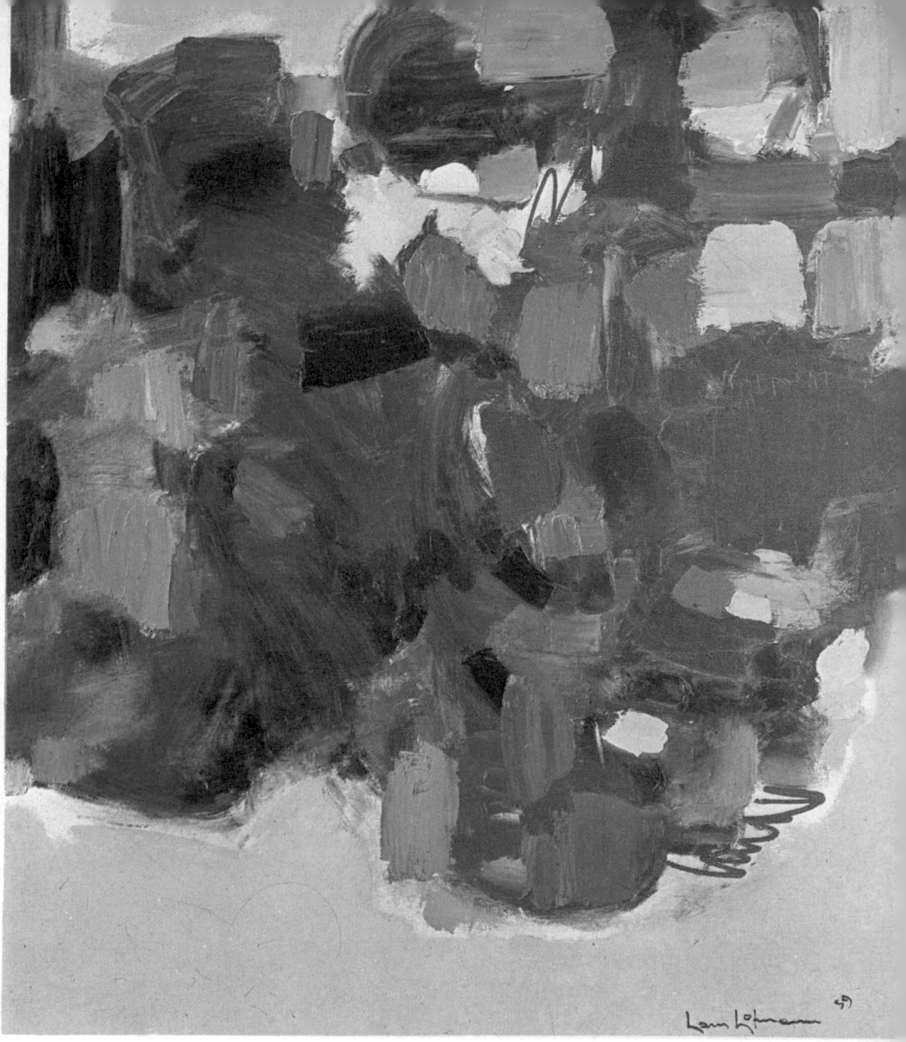

180. ***Emerald Isle*****, by Hans Hofmann**

their free, intuitive compositions (Plate 180). His influence on other media has also been extensive.

Robert Motherwell (1915–   ), another of the American abstractionists, retains a firm clarity of outline in his free geometric shapes, usually painted in bold flat colors. In his compositions, there is a greater awareness of traditional rules of artistic balance; and in works such as *The Dance* (Plate 181), one finds a suggestion of the geometric purity and sensitive arrangement of Jean Arp's

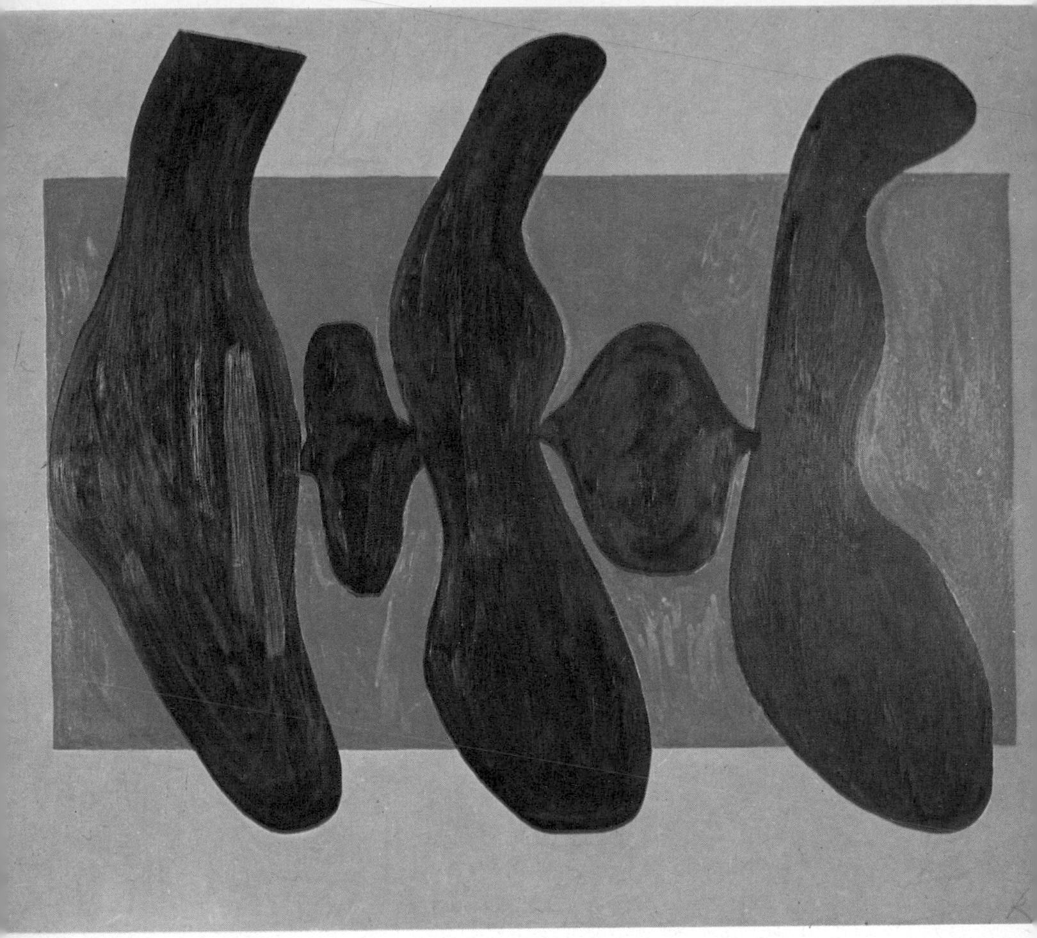

181. ***The Dance,*** **by Robert Motherwell**

painted reliefs or of Matisse's colored-paper cutouts. And, in fact, Motherwell has often adopted the collage as a preferred medium.

The work of Willem de Kooning (1904–　　), like that of Gorky, reflects its heritage. He is able to absorb thoughtfully the achievements of earlier painters and continually experiments with elements from the artistic past. "There is," he has said, "a train track in the history of art that goes back to Mesopotamia." De Kooning's pictures are often frantic and violent. Violence is

182. ***Woman on a Bicycle,*** **by Willem de Kooning**

evident in the slashing quality of the brushwork itself (Plate 182). The emphasis on the act of painting as something having meaning and existence in itself—already described among the French tachists—has also characterized many New York artists in the post-World War II period. It is for this reason they are called "action painters." In De Kooning's work such "action" is apparent in the slurred paint, the broken line, and fragmented forms. His paintings, sometimes totally and sometimes only partly abstract, are often huge in scale.

The painting of large pictures was another trait common to most of the New York action painters. A big picture demands a response from the spectator. Some of the largest modern American paintings are those of the most famous action painter, Jackson Pollock. Some are sixteen feet long. Until about 1946 a more or less postcubist painter, Pollock combined certain cubist traditions with elements of Miró, Hans Hofmann, and the Mexican muralist José Clemente Orozco (1883–1949). From this blend of styles he created a completely new way of painting. He was a supreme master of line; in his greatest works of the late 1940's (Plate 183), the dribbled threads of line cross and recross the canvas in endless loops and swirls. The whole picture consists of an intricate network of lines.

Pollock's line differs from that of Gorky or Matta in that it is not an instrument of drawing, in the sense of descriptive representation. In conventional drawing, a line defines a form, a silhouette, or a division. Pollock's achievement was to free line from these traditional functions. Pollock used lines, blobs, and even occasional handprints to create a purely visual experience. These elements are never made to function as signs or symbols in his compositions, instead, they exist for their own sake. The content of the picture becomes the material form itself—neither more nor less.

The New York painters of the post-war decades are often called "abstract expressionists," a term that is misleading in many cases. In Pollock's work, for instance, there is no perceptible "expression" of the familiar whatsoever. Action paintings are not in-

183. ***Number 1,*** **by Jackson Pollock**
184. ***Forms Following Man,*** **by Mark Tobey**

185. ***Flight of Plover,*** **by Morris Graves**

tended as *pictures* of things, but as tangible emotional experiences as *things* in themselves.

The work of Mark Tobey (1890–   ) illustrates another strand running through American painting: the influence of the Far East and Oriental culture. Tobey's pictures, like Pollock's, rely principally on line and have no particularly emphasized areas. While in the Orient, he found that he could "write" his feelings in layer upon layer of endless calligraphy (the art of handwriting or penmanship; also, Oriental script). Back in America, during and after World War II, he made the "White Writing" series for which he is famous. This delicate style of calligraphic painting can be seen in *Forms Following Man* (Plate 184).

Like Tobey, Morris Graves (1910–   ) is a visionary painter. He has studied Oriental philosophies and religions in his search for the essence of life and nature. His paintings, most often of bird themes, clearly reflect his mystical absorption in nature, one poetic example being the breathtaking expressive *Flight of Plover* (Plate 185).

186. *The Scarecrow*, by Andrew Wyeth

187. ***Red, White, and Brown,*** **by Mark Rothko**

Another acute observer of nature, Andrew Wyeth (1917–), is technically the most accomplished present-day naturalistic painter in the United States. He has devoted his life to portraying the people and the countryside of his native eastern Pennsylvania. The son of a famous illustrator, Wyeth developed his meticulously realistic technique quite early. He applies his microscopic brushwork to haunting, mournful landscapes (Plate 186) and thoughtful portraits.

Mark Rothko (1903–1970), a master of color, passed through a phase of late surrealism before arriving at what is the purest, most simplified painting of the time in his distinctive abstract works (Plate 187). His great canvases of the late 1940's and 1950's are enormous, almost bare expanses of color in which subject matter has been reduced to a minimum. What remains is the glowing activity of two or three colors.

Franz Kline (1910–1962) drew incessantly on telephone books, menus, and letters—in an attempt to capture on paper the dynamism of life. His powerful black-and-white paintings (Plate 188), without the help of color, depend, as one critic admiringly remarked, "solely on the weighted brushstroke, the thick or thin, shiny or matte [dull] streaks of black and white pigment. . . ." Kline himself declared that the final test of painting is: "Does the emotion come across?" This must be the basis of his paintings—

188. ***Buttress,*** **by Franz Kline**

189. ***Small Rebus,*** **by Robert Rauschenberg**

action and emotion. Even he refused to explain them, saying, "The first works in only black and white seemed related to figures, and I titled them as such. Later the results seemed to signify something—but difficult to give subject [or] name to, and at present I find it impossible to make a direct verbal statement about the paintings in white and black."

The New York artists of the postwar decade started yet another revolution in painting. In some respects the innovations and achievements of the abstract expressionists have proved to be dead ends, but not through any weakness of their own. It was simply that some of their art was unique and, therefore, showed no way forward as a consistent movement. In other ways, however, they opened new areas of advance for painters. Pollock's action painting was such a final triumph and proved so individual that his followers have seemed merely imitators, and few have successfully continued his work. The varieties of total abstraction established by Kline, Rothko, and Tobey, nevertheless, have become a basis from which artists both good and bad could proceed. An art so thoroughly stripped of all that was inessential could well absorb new subject matter and concerns—as indeed it has done, and will continue to do.

In the 1960's, a new generation of painters and sculptors emerged upon the American scene; and, seemingly overnight, their innovative works were neatly categorized and labeled by art dealers and critics for the benefit of a novelty-hungry public. Dissatisfied with the emotional and technical ambiguities of Abstract Expressionism, this new wave of artists focused their attention upon clearly definable forms such as the trappings of a vulgarized consumer society, in the case of "Pop Art"; or on geometric figures and "hard-edged" shapes, in the case of "the new abstraction" and "Op Art" (implying experimentation with optical illusion).

Prior to the resounding international success of Pop Art, a success hopelessly inflated by the sort of publicity usually reserved by the news media for popular singing idols and movie stars, the field of "commercial art," typified by illustrations for advertisements, had been held in utter contempt by practitioners of "fine art"—artists who intended their works to grace museums, galleries, and private collections—never the pages of a cheap magazine or the back of a soap box. With an almost perverse glee, however, Pop Artists now seized upon the slick techniques and banal subject matter of the despised "commercial art" and cheerfully set about reprocessing them into "fine art." Accordingly, faithful reproductions of soup cans and cola bottles suddenly could be found displayed in galleries along with sprawling plastic hamburgers, billboard close-ups, stencil lettering, comic strip heroines, and all the other paraphanalia of "commercial art." The leading figures of the Pop movement include within its vaguely outlined boundaries Andy Warhol (Plate 190), Class Oldenburg, James Rosenquist, George Segal, Marisol, Larry Rivers, Roy

Lichtenstein, Jasper Johns, Jim Dine, Tom Wesselman, Robert Indiana, and Robert Rauschenberg. Rauschenberg speaking, about a technical point once stated that "A picture is more like the real world when it is made out of the real world."

190. ***Green Coca-Cola Bottles,*** **by Andy Warho**

Viewing art as a "matter of just accepting whatever happens," he sees the act of creation as mainly a "collaboration" with the real external world. And what better way to depict this world than with actual items taken from it. Cubist and futurist collages had employed this technique, but usually for simple purposes of allusion—for instance, to suggest the life of the café or the spirit of music and the theater. In more recent work such as Rauschenberg's *Small Rebus* (Plate 189), however, these real components are put together with an eye to odd juxtapositions and a jarring removal from their original contexts. In his "combines" of pasted paper, bits of wood, photographs, oil paint on canvas, and other objects, Rauschenberg presents a fragmented view of reality that can be humorous and sardonic or shocking and condemnatory in effect. Artists most frequently associated with "the new abstraction" include Frank Stella, Larry Poons, Ellsworth Kelly.

191. ***Scissors Jack Series,* by Larry Zox**

Kenneth Noland, and Larry Zox (Plate 191). Their strictly regimented areas of flat, strikingly arranged art upon both rectangular and eccentrically-shaped canvases, have breathed new life into the tradition of purely abstract painting.

A recent and unfortunate trend seems to have been set by the art world's compulsion to annually herald the birth of an "important new movement." This tendency to worship the new, no matter what its true worth, is a dangerous one and should be shunned in the interest of future art. In the words of Henry Moore, "Art is not fashion but evolution!" and it is only from the vantage point of time that the real importance of any artistic movement can be assessed. For this reason the long-term effects of both Pop Art and the New Abstraction upon the fascinating course of the 20th century are yet to be conclusively observed.

LIST OF ILLUSTRATIONS

39. *Contrast of Forms,* by Fernand Léger. Musée d'Art Moderne, Paris.
40. *Still Life with Bottles and a Knife,* by Juan Gris. Rijksmuseum Kröller-Müller, Otterlo (Netherlands).
41. *Still Life with Fruit Dish and Water Bottle,* by Juan Gris. Rijksmuseum Kröller-Müller, Otterlo (Netherlands).
42. *Women Sewing,* by Albert Gleizes. Rijksmuseum Kröller-Müller, Otterlo (Netherlands).
43. *Still Life,* by Jean Metzinger. Metropolitan Museum of Art, New York.
44. *Le Passage de la Vierge à la Mariée,* by Marcel Duchamp. Museum of Modern Art, New York.
45. *Oval,* by Robert Delaunay. Peggy Guggenheim Collection, Venice.
46. *Arrangement in Verticals,* by Frank Kupka. Musée d'Art Moderne, Paris.
47. *Head of a Woman,* by Pablo Picasso. Kunsthaus, Zurich.
48. *Portrait of Marthe Girieud,* by Henri Laurens. Gallery Louis Leiris, Paris.
49. *Pierrot Carrousel,* by Alexander Archipenko. Solomon R. Guggenheim Museum, New York.
50. *Dancer,* by Jacques Lipchitz. Museum of the Petit Palais, Paris.
51. *Horse,* by Raymond Duchamp-Villon. Musée d'Art Moderne, Paris.
52. *Unique Forms of Continuity in Space,* by Umberto Boccioni. Galleria d'Arte Moderna, Milan.
53. *The Riot in the Galleria,* by Umberto Boccioni. Private collection, Milan.
54. *What the Tram Said to Me,* by Carlo Carra. Private collection, Milan.
55. *Dancer in Blue,* by Gino Severini. Private collection, Milan.
56. *Little Girl Running on the Balcony,* by Giacomo Balla. Galleria d'Arte Moderna, Milan.
57. *Dynamism of a Cyclist,* by Umberto Boccioni. Private collection, Milan.
58. *Pursuit,* by Carlo Carrà. Private collection, Milan.
59. *Patriotic Celebration,* by Carlo Carrà. Private collection, Milan.
60. *Self-portrait with a Model,* 1907 by Ernst Ludwig Kirchner. Kunsthalle, Hamburg.
61. *Forest,* by Karl Schmidt-Rottluff. Kunsthalle, Hamburg.
62. *Two Men Seated at a Table,* by Erich Heckel. Kunsthalle, Hamburg.
63. *Children in a Wood,* by Otto Müller. Kunsthalle, Hamburg.
64. *Garden with Red and Yellow Roses,* by Emil Nolde. Wallraf-Richartz Museum, Cologne (Germany).
65. *Dancers,* by Emil Nolde. Staatsgalerie, Stuttgart (Germany).
66. *Portrait of Edith, the Artist's Wife,* by Egon Schiele. Österreichische Galerie, Vienna.
67. *Portrait of Professor Auguste Farel,* by Oskar Kokoschka. Städtische Kunsthalle, Mannheim (Germany).
68. *The Heathen,* by Oskar Kokoschka. Wallraf-Richartz Museum, Cologne (Germany).
69. *Crinolines,* by Vassily Kandinsky. Solomon R. Guggenheim Museum, New York.
70. *Paradise,* by Vassily Kandinsky. Private collection, Turin.
71. *With the Black Arch,* by Vassily Kandinsky. Collection of Mme Kandinsky, Paris.
72. *Separation,* by August Macke. Wallraf-Richartz Museum, Cologne.
73. *Still Life,* by Alexei von Jawlensky. Wallraf-Richartz Museum, Cologne.
74. *The White Plume,* by Alexei von Jawlensky. Staatgalerie, Stuttgart (Germany).
75. *Composition in Line and Color,* by Piet Mondrian. Rijksmuseum Kröller-Müller, Otterlo (Netherlands).
76. *Geometric Composition,* by Theo van Doesburg. Rijksmuseum Kröller-Müller, Otterlo (Netherlands).
77. *Geometric Composition II,* by Bart van der Leck. Rijksmuseum Kröller-Müller, Otterlo (Netherlands).

78. *Composition with Red, Yellow, and Blue,* by Piet Mondrian. Gemeentemuseum, The Hague (Netherlands).
79. *Woman with a Tie,* by Amedeo Modigliani. Private collection, Paris.
80. *Head,* by Amedeo Modigliani. Solomon R. Guggenheim Museum, New York.
81. *Dead Fowl,* by Chaim Soutine. Musée d'Art Moderne, Paris.
82. *The Pageboy at Maxim's,* by Chaim Soutine. Private collection, Paris.
83. *Mirelle,* by Jules Pascin. Musée d'Art Moderne, Paris.
84. *Rue Norvins,* by Maurice Utrillo. Kunsthaus, Zurich.
85. *Interior with Goldfish,* by Henri Matisse. Museum of Modern Art, New York.
86. *Decorative Figure on an Ornamental Background,* by Henri Matisse. Musée d'Art Moderne, Paris.
87. *Jeannette IV,* by Henri Matisse. Museum of Modern Art, New York.
88. *The Paris Òpera House,* by Raoul Dufy. Phillips Collection, Washington, D.C.
89. *Two Sisters,* by André Derain. Statens Museum for Kunst, Copenhagen.
90. *Harlequin at the Looking Glass,* by Pablo Picasso. Private collection, Izuyama (Japan).
91. *The Muse,* by Pablo Picasso. Musée d'Art Moderne, Paris.
92. *Guernica* (detail), by Pablo Picasso. Museum of Modern Art, New York (on loan from the artist).
93. *The Mexican War of Independence,* by Diego Rivera. Palacio Nacional, Mexico City.
94. *Echo of a Scream,* by David Alfaro Siqueiros. Museum of Modern Art, New York.
95. *Still Life on a Marble Table,* by Georges Braque. Musée d'Art Moderne, Paris.
96. *Wheat Field,* by Georges Braque. Private collection, Zurich.
97. *Soldiers Playing Cards,* by Fernand Legér. Rijksmuseum Kröller-Müller, Otterlo (Netherlands).
98. *Leisure: Homage to Louis David,* by Fernand Léger. Musée d'Art Moderne, Paris.
99. *Paris through the Window,* by Marc Chagall. Solomon R. Guggenheim Museum, New York.
100. *To My Wife,* by Marc Chagall. Musée d'Art Moderne, Paris.
101. *The Twittering Machine,* by Paul Klee. Museum of Modern Art, New York.
102. *Highways and Byways,* by Paul Klee. Wallraf-Richartz Museum, Cologne (Germany).
103. *Still Life,* by Giorgio Morandi. Private collection, Milan.
104. *Still Life with Manikin,* by Giorgio Morandi. Private collection, Milan.
105. *Nostalgia of the Poet,* by Giorgio de Chirico. Peggy Guggenheim Collection, Venice.
106. *Hector and Andromache,* by Giorgio de Chirico. Private collection, Milan.
107. *The Hermaphrodite Idol,* by Carlo Carrà. Private collection, Milan.
108. *Composition,* 1926 by Kurt Schwitters. Private collection, Rome.
109. *L'Enfant Carburateur,* by Francis Picabia. Solomon R. Guggenheim Museum, New York.
110. *The Bride Stripped Bare by Her Bachelors, Even,* by Marcel Duchamp. Museum of Art, Philadelphia.
111. *The Eye of Silence,* by Max Ernst. Washington University Art Collections, St. Louis.
112. *Large Composition,* by Joan Miró. Private collection, Milan.
113. *Man and Dog in Front of the Sun,* by Joan Miró. Öffentliche Kunstsammlung, Basel (Switzerland).
114. *Premonition of Civil War,* by Salvador Dali. Museum of Art, Philadelphia.
115. *Fear,* 1949 by Yves Tanguy. Oil on canvas 60 × 40″. Collection Whitney Museum of American Art, New York.
116. *Voice of the Winds,* by René Magritte. Peggy Guggenheim Collection, Venice.

117. *Perspective: Madame Récamier of Gérard,* by René Magritte. Private collection, Milan.
118. *Human Concretion,* by Jean Arp. Kunsthaus, Zurich.
119. *The Piazza,* by Alberto Giacometti. Öffentliche Kunstsammlung, Basel (Switzerland).
120. *The Forest,* by Alberto Giacometti. Private collection, Paris.
121. *Hercules Aiming at the Stymphalian Birds,* by Emile Antoine Bourdelle. Metropolitan Museum of Art, New York.
122. *Venus with a Necklace,* by Aristide Maillol. Kunsthaus, Zurich.
123. *Paulette,* by Charles Despiau. Musée d'Art Moderne, Paris.
124. *Man Singing,* by Ernst Barlach. Kunsthalle, Mannheim (Germany).
125. *Kneeling Woman,* by Wilhelm Lehmbruck. Museum of Modern Art, New York.
126. *The Maiastra,* by Constantin Brancusi. Peggy Guggenheim Collection, Venice.
127. *Sleeping Muse,* by Constantin Brancusi. Musée d'Art Moderne, Paris.
128. *Adam and Eve,* by Constantin Brancuse. Solomon R. Guggenheim Museum, New York.
129. *Construction in an Egg,* by Antoine Pevsner. Private collection, Paris.
130. *Woman Combing Her Hair,* by Julio González. Musée d'Art Moderne, Paris.
131. *Maternity,* by Pablo Gargallo. Private collection, Paris.
132. *Monument Commemorating the Destruction of Rotterdam,* by Ossip Zadkine. Rotterdam (outdoor).
133. *Sacrifice II,* 1948–52 bronze 49¼″ high by Jacques Lipchitz. Collection Whitney Museum of American Art, New York.
134. *Return of the Son,* by Jacques Lipchitz. Solomon R. Guggenheim Museum, New York.
135. *The Visitation,* by Sir Jacob Epstein. Tate Gallery, London.
136. *Selina,* by Sir Jacob Epstein. Brooklyn Museum, New York.
137. *Reclining Figure,* by Henry Moore. Tate Gallery, London.
138. *Warrior,* by Henry Moore. Kunsthalle, Mannheim (Germany).
139. *The Rocking Chair,* by Henry Moore. City Museum and Art Gallery, Birmingham (England).
140. *Two Figures (Menhir),* by Barbara Hepworth. Gimpel Sons Ltd., London.
141. *Two Standing Figures,* (1950), by Kenneth Armitage. Gimpel Sons Ltd., London.
142. *Mobile,* by Alexander Calder. Galleria Blu, Milan.
143. *The Great Spider,* by Alexander Calder. Öffentliche Kunstsammlung, Basel (Switzerland).
144. *Sun Image I,* by Louise Nevelson. Hannover Gallery, London.
145. *Kouros,* by Isamu Noguchi. Metropolitan Museum of Art—Fletcher Fund 1953, New York.
146. *Sea Sentinel,* Steel and bronze 105″ high 1956 by Theodore Roszak. Collection Whitney Museum of American Art, New York.
147. *Artist and Model,* by Giacomo Manzu. Galleria Galatea, Turin.
148. *Horse and Rider,* by Marino Marini. Private collection, Turin.
149. *The Funeral of the Poet Panizza,* by George Grosz. Staatsgaleria, Stuttgart, The Estate of George Grosz, Princeton, N.J.
150. *Metropolis,* by George Grosz. 1917 Museum of Modern Art, New York. The Estate of George Grosz, Princeton, N.J.
151. *Two Women,* by Max Beckmann. Wallraf-Richartz Museum, Cologne (Germany).
152. *The Departure,* by Max Beckmann. Museum of Modern Art, New York.
153. *The Sailor Brothers,* by Constant Permeke. Öffentliche Kunstsammlung, Basel (Switzerland).
154. *The Lottery,* by Marcel Gromaire. Musée d'Art Moderne, Paris.
155. *The Suburb,* by Mario Sironi. Private collection, Milan.
156. *Peonies,* by Filippo de Pisis. Private collection, Milan.

157. *Evening Offering,* by Alfred Manessier. Musée d'Art Moderne, Paris.
158. *Le Lavandou,* by Nicolas de Staël. Musée d'Art Moderne, Paris.
159. *The Financial and Economic System,* by Georges Mathieu. Private collection, Milan.
160. *February 9,* by Pierre Soulages. Kunsthaus, Zurich.
161. *Rue Brise Elan,* by Jean Dubuffet. Collection of the artist, Paris.
162. *Portrait of Edith Boissonnas,* by Jean Dubuffet. Galleria del Naviglio, Milan.
163. *Portrait of Van Gough,* by Francis Bacon. Tate Gallery, London.
164. *Thorn Trees,* by Graham Sutherland. Albright-Knox Art Gallery, Buffalo, N.Y.
165. *Haymarket,* by John Sloan. The Brooklyn Museum, New York. Gift of Mrs. Harry Payne Whitney.
166. *The Solitary Tenement,* by George Bellows. National Gallery of Art, Washington, D.C. Gift of Chester Dale.
167. *Brooklyn Bridge, Variations on an old theme,* 1939 by Joseph Stella. Oil on canvas 70 × 42″. Collection Whitney Museum of American Art, New York.
168. *Quoddy Head, Maine Coast,* by John Marin. Phillips Collection, Washington, D.C.
169. *American Gothic,* 1930 by Grant Wood. Courtesy of the Art Institute, Chicago.
170. *House of Mystery,* by Charles Burchfield. The Art Institute, Chicago.
171. *Night Café,* by Edward Hopper. The Art Institute, Chicago.
172. *Flour Mill Abstraction,* by Arthur G. Dove. Phillips Collection, Washington, D.C.
173. *The Paris Bit* 1959, by Stuart Davis. Oil on canvas 46 × 60″. Collection Whitney Museum of American Art, New York.
174. *Welcome Home!* by Jack Levine. Brooklyn Museum, New York.
175. *Lily and the Sparrows,* 1939 Oil on composition board 30 × 49″, by Philip Evergood. Collection Whitney Museum of American Art, New York.
176. *The Passion of Sacco and Vanzetti,* 1931–32 From the series of 23 paintings of Sacco-vanzetti Tempra on canvas 84½ × 48″, by Ben Shahn. Collection Whitney Museum of American Art, New York. By courtesy of Kennedy Galleries.
177. *Betrothal II,* by Arshile Gorky. 1947 Oil on canvas 50¾ × 38″. Collection Whitney Museum of American Art, New York.
178. *Removal of the Cards,* by Roberto Matta (Echaurren). Galerie du Dragon, Paris.
179. *The Waiting Room,* by George Tooker. Johnson Collection, Museum of Art, Philadelphia.
180. *Emerald Isle,* 1959 by Hans Hofmann. Smithsonian Institute, Washington, D.C.
181. *The Dance,* by Robert Motherwell. Metropolitan Museum of Art, New York.
182. *Woman on a Bicycle,* 1952–53 Oil on canvas 76½ × 49″, by Willem de Kooning. Collection Whitney Museum of American Art, New York.
183. *Number 1,* by Jackson Pollock. Museum of Modern Art, New York.
184. *Forms Following Man,* by Mark Tobey. Fuller Collection, Art Museum, Seattle.
185. *Flight of Plover,* 1955 by Morris Graves. Oil on composition board 36 × 48″. Collection Whitney Museum of American Art, New York.
186. *The Scarecrow,* by Andrew Wyeth. Johnson Collection, Museum of Art, Philadelphia.
187. *Red, White, and Brown,* by Mark Rothko. Öffentliche Kunstsammlung, Basel (Switzerland).
188. *Buttress,* by Franz Kline. Private collection Varese (Italy).

189. *Small Rebus,* by Robert Rauschenberg. Private collection, Varese (Italy).

190. *Green Coca-Cola Bottles,* (1962), by Andy Warhol (208.5 × 267 cm). Whitney Museum of American Art, New York.

191. *Scissors Jack Series,* (1965–66), by Larry Zox. Kornblee Gallery, New York.

INDEX